The Wiersbe
BIBLE STUDY SERIES

PSALMS

The
Wiersbe
BIBLE STUDY SERIES

Glorifying God

for Who He Is

David C Cook®
transforming lives together

THE WIERSBE BIBLE STUDY SERIES: PSALMS
Published by David C. Cook
4050 Lee Vance View
Colorado Springs, CO 80918 U.S.A.

David C. Cook Distribution Canada
55 Woodslee Avenue, Paris, Ontario, Canada N3L 3E5

David C. Cook U.K., Kingsway Communications
Eastbourne, East Sussex BN23 6NT, England

David C. Cook and the graphic circle C logo
are registered trademarks of Cook Communications Ministries.

The Web site addresses recommended throughout this book are offered as a
resource to you. These Web sites are not intended in any way to be or imply an
endorsement on the part of David C. Cook, nor do we vouch for their content.

All excerpts taken from *Be Worshipful*, second edition, published by David C. Cook in 2009
© 2004 Warren W. Wiersbe, ISBN 978-1-4347-6739-4; and *Be Exultant*, second edition,
published by David C. Cook in 2009 © 2004 Warren W. Wiersbe, ISBN 978-1-4347-6737-0.

ISBN 978-1-4347-6487-4
eISBN 978-0-7814-0491-4

© 2010 Warren W. Wiersbe

The Team: Steve Parolini, Karen Lee-Thorp, Amy Kiechlin,
Sarah Schultz, Jack Campbell, and Karen Athen
Series Cover Design: John Hamilton Design
Cover Photo: iStockphoto

Printed in the United States of America
First Edition 2010

1 2 3 4 5 6 7 8 9 10

042710

Contents

Introduction to Psalms

The Name

The book of Psalms has been and still is the irreplaceable devotional guide, prayer book, and hymnal of the people of God. The Hebrew title is "the book of praises" (*tehillim*). The Greek translation of the Old Testament (the Septuagint) used *psalmos* for *tehillim;* the word means "a song sung to the accompaniment of a stringed instrument." The Vulgate followed the Septuagint and used *psalmorum*, from the Latin *psalterium*, "a stringed instrument." The King James Version adopted the word, and thus we have the book of Psalms.

The Writers

The writers of about two-thirds of the psalms are identified in the superscriptions. David leads the way with seventy-three psalms. He was Israel's beloved "singer of songs" (2 Sam. 23:1) and the man who organized the temple ministry, including the singers (1 Chron. 15:16; 16:7; 25:1). The sons of Korah, who served as musicians in the temple (1 Chron. 6:31ff.; 15:17ff.; 2 Chron. 20:19), wrote eleven psalms (42—49; 84—85; 87), Asaph twelve psalms (50; 73—83), King Solomon two (72; 127), Ethan one (89), and Moses one (90). However, not all scholars give equal value to the titles of the psalms.

The Structure

The book of Psalms is divided into five books, perhaps in imitation of the five books of Moses (Genesis—Deuteronomy): 1—41; 42—72; 73—89; 90—106; 107—150. Each of the first three books ends with a double "amen," the fourth ends with an "amen" and a "hallelujah," and the last book closes the entire collection with a "hallelujah." The book of Psalms grew over the years as the Holy Spirit directed different writers and editors to compose and compile these songs and poems.

The Purpose

Primarily, the Psalms are about God and His relationship to His creation, the nations of the world, Israel, and His believing people. He is seen as a powerful God as well as a tenderhearted Father, a God who keeps His promises and lovingly cares for His people. The Psalms also reveal the hearts of those who follow Him, their faith and doubts, their victories and failures, and their hopes for the glorious future God has promised.

In the book of Psalms, you meet the God of creation and learn spiritual truths from birds and beasts, mountains and deserts, sunshine and storms, wheat and chaff, trees and flowers. The psalms teach us to seek God with a whole heart, to tell Him the truth and tell Him everything, and to worship Him because of who He is, not just because of what He gives. They show us how to accept trials and turn them into triumphs, and when we've failed, they show us how to repent and receive God's gracious forgiveness.

The God described in the book of Psalms is both immanent and transcendent, far above us and yet personally with us in our pilgrim journey. He is "God Most High" and "Immanuel—God with us."

—*Warren W. Wiersbe*

How to Use This Study

This study is designed for both individual and small-group use. It is divided into twelve lessons—each focuses on selected psalms and references one or more sections in Warren W. Wiersbe's commentaries *Be Worshipful* and *Be Exultant* (second editions, David C. Cook, 2009). While reading the commentaries is not a prerequisite for going through this study, the additional insights and background Wiersbe offers can greatly enhance your study experience.

The Getting Started questions at the beginning of each lesson offer you an opportunity to record your first thoughts and reactions to the study text. This is an important step in the study process as those "first impressions" often include clues about what it is your heart is longing to discover.

The bulk of the study is found in the Going Deeper questions. These dive into the Bible text and, along with helpful excerpts from Wiersbe's commentary, help you examine not only the original context and meaning of the verses but also modern application.

Looking Inward narrows the focus down to your personal story. These intimate questions can be a bit uncomfortable at times, but don't shy away from honesty here. This is where you are asked to stand before the mirror of God's Word and look closely at what you see. It's the place to take a good look at yourself in light of the lesson and search for ways in which you can grow in faith.

Going Forward is the place where you can commit to paper those things you want or need to do in order to better live out the discoveries you made in the Looking Inward section. Don't skip or skim through this. Take the time to really consider what practical steps you might take to move closer to Christ. Then share your thoughts with a trusted friend who can act as an encourager and accountability partner.

Finally, there is a brief Seeking Help section to close the lesson. This is a reminder for you to invite God into your spiritual-growth process. If you choose to write out a prayer in this section, come back to it as you work through the lesson and continue to seek the Holy Spirit's guidance as you discover God's will for your life.

Tips for Small Groups

A small group is a dynamic thing. One week it might seem like a group of close-knit friends. The next it might seem more like a group of uncomfortable strangers. A small-group leader's role is to read these subtle changes and adjust the tone of the discussion accordingly.

Small groups need to be safe places for people to talk openly. It is through shared wrestling with difficult life issues that some of the greatest personal growth is discovered. But in order for the group to feel safe, participants need to know it's okay *not* to share sometimes. Always invite honest disclosure, but never force someone to speak if he or she isn't comfortable doing so. (A savvy leader will follow up later with a group member who isn't comfortable sharing in a group setting to see if a one-on-one discussion is more appropriate.)

Have volunteers take turns reading excerpts from Scripture or from the commentary. The more each person is involved even in the mundane tasks, the more they'll feel comfortable opening up in more meaningful ways.

The leader should watch the clock and keep the discussion moving. Sometimes there may be more Going Deeper questions than your group can cover in your available time. If you've had a fruitful discussion, it's okay to move on without finishing everything. And if you think the group is getting bogged down on a question or has taken off on a tangent, you can simply say, "Let's go on to question 5." Be sure to save at least ten to fifteen minutes for the Going Forward questions.

Finally, soak your group meetings in prayer—before you begin, during as needed, and always at the end of your time together.

Wisdom, Prophecy, and Lament

(PSALMS 1—3)

Before you begin ...

- *Pray for the Holy Spirit to reveal truth and wisdom as you go through this lesson.*
- *Read Psalms 1—3. This lesson references content in* Be Worshipful. *It will be helpful for you to have your Bible and a copy of the commentary available as you work through this lesson.*

Getting Started

From the Commentary

Psalm 1 is a wisdom psalm and focuses on God's Word, God's blessing on those who obey it and meditate on it, and God's ultimate judgment on those who rebel. Wisdom psalms also wrestle with the problem of evil in the world and why God permits the prosperity of the wicked who reject His law.... While this psalm depicts two ways, it actually describes three different persons and how they relate to the blessing of the Lord.

—*Be Worshipful*, pages 19–20

1. What makes this a "wisdom" psalm? What wisdom is being presented? Who are the three different persons described in this brief psalm?

Concentrate on God's Word

The Righteous
the sinner
the Wicked

the psalms were written By the Jews So only the Jews could be the Righteous

the gentiles were the sinners

we know the wicked all of us.

More to Consider: Read another wisdom psalm, such as Psalm 10, 12, 15, or 19. What is the wisdom being presented in each of these psalms? How is this wisdom applicable to Christians today?

2. Choose one verse or phrase from Psalms 1—3 that stands out to you. This could be something you're intrigued by, something that makes you uncomfortable, something that puzzles you, something that resonates with you, or just something you want to examine further. Write that here.

Psa 1:8 Salvation belongs to the Lord may your blessings Be upon your People Psa 3:8

Going Deeper

From the Commentary

[handwritten, left margin: Is this about the Psalms?]

[handwritten, above text: we are Not Israel]

God's covenant with Israel made it clear that He would bless their obedience and judge their disobedience (Lev. 26; Deut. 28). The word *blessed* is *asher,* the name of one of Jacob's sons (Gen. 30:12–13). It's plural: "O the happinesses! O the blessednesses!" The person described in verses 1–2 met the conditions and therefore God blessed him. If we want God's blessings, we, too, must meet the conditions.

—*Be Worshipful,* page 20

3. According to Psalm 1:1–2, what are the conditions we must meet in order to be blessed by God? How do we go about meeting those conditions? What sort of person is described in Psalm 1:4–5? What are the consequences for those who do not meet the conditions described in Psalm 1:1–2?

[handwritten:]
Does not follow the advise of the wicked
or takes the path of the sinners
Does not join the mockers

Instead
He Delights in the Lords instructions
and meditates on the Lords
instruction day and night.

From the Commentary

> This psalm begins with "blessed" and ends with "perish."
> True believers are blessed in Christ (Eph. 1:3ff.). They
> have received God's blessing, and they ought to be a bless-
> ing to others, especially to the chaff that will one day be
> thrown into the fire.
>
> —*Be Worshipful*, page 23

4. What is a believer's responsibility to "the wicked" (v. 6)? How does
being blessed by God help believers reach out to those who are otherwise
destined to "perish" (v. 6)? What practical implications does this have for
Christians today?

From Today's World

A Google search of the word *wisdom* turns up a diverse listing of links—
everything from "wisdom quotes" to Buddhist books. And for many people
today, the self-help section of the bookstore is the only place where they
expect to find wisdom. While certainly a step up from the proclamations
found in fortune cookies, random Internet links and self-help books still

fall short of providing answers to the significant life questions that send people to them in the first place.

5. What prompts people to seek out wisdom? Why do the secular answers fall short of providing what they're looking for? How can the wisdom found in Psalms (and Proverbs) provide the missing pieces? What is the key difference between worldly wisdom and biblical wisdom?

From the Commentary

Psalm 1 emphasizes God's law, while Psalm 2 focuses on prophecy. The people in Psalm 1 delight in the law, but the people in Psalm 2 defy the law. Psalm 1 begins with a beatitude, and Psalm 2 ends with a beatitude. Psalm 1 is never quoted in the New Testament, while Psalm 2 is quoted or alluded to at least seventeen times, more than any single psalm.

—*Be Worshipful,* page 23

6. Why do you think Psalm 2 is quoted so often in the New Testament? What about the psalm makes it so quote worthy? (See Matt. 3:17; 17:5, for

examples.) What is the beatitude (blessing) that ends Psalm 2? Why is it significant that Psalm 2 ends with a beatitude? How does the message of this beatitude compare to the beatitude that opens Psalm 1?

From the Commentary

> David didn't expect a reply when he asked the question in Psalm 2:1, because there really is no reply. It was an expression of astonishment: "When you consider all that the Lord has done for the nations, how can they rebel against Him!" God had provided for their basic needs (Acts 14:15–17), guided them, kept them alive, and sent a Savior to bring forgiveness and eternal life (Acts 17:24–31; see Dan. 4:32). Yet, from the Tower of Babel (Gen. 11) to the crucifixion of Christ (Acts 4:21–31) to the battle of Armageddon (Rev. 19:11ff.), the Bible records humanity's foolish and futile rebellions against the will of the Creator.
>
> —*Be Worshipful*, page 24

7. What does it mean that the Lord "scoffs" at the kings of the earth? In what ways are the kings' rebellion directly against the Messiah, Jesus

Christ? What is it about the Messiah's coming reign that causes the kings to rebel? How and where is that mind-set still prevalent today?

From the Commentary

In view of the Father's decree and promised judgment, and the Son's victorious enthronement in heaven, the wise thing for people to do is to surrender to Christ and trust Him. Today, the Spirit of God speaks to mankind and pleads with sinners to repent and turn to the Savior.

Note that in verses 10 and 11, the Spirit speaks first to the kings and leaders, and then in verse 12, He addresses "all" and urges them to trust the Son.

—*Be Worshipful,* page 26

8. Why do you think the Spirit speaks first to the kings and leaders in Psalm 2:10–11? Why was this particularly significant for the culture of the day when the psalm was written? Is it also applicable today? Why or why not? What keeps people from doing the "wise" thing as directed in this psalm?

More to Consider: In the ancient world, vassal rulers would show their obedience to their king by kissing his hand or cheek. This is the kiss of submission and even reconciliation. How does this describe the kiss referred to in Psalm 2:12?

From the Commentary

Psalm 3 is the first time we find the word *psalm* in the book. The Hebrew word is *mizmor* and means "to pluck strings." This is also the first prayer in the Psalms and the first psalm attributed to David. All the psalms in book 1 (Ps. 1—41) are attributed to David except 1; 10; and 33. (Ps. 2 is assigned to him in Acts 4:25.) Psalm 3 is categorized as a "personal lament," and there are many of these in the collection.... David wrote the psalm after he had fled Jerusalem when his son Absalom took over the throne (2 Sam. 15—18). The king and his attendants had crossed the Jordan River and camped at Mahanaim. This is a morning psalm (v. 5).

—*Be Worshipful,* pages 27–28

9. What makes Psalm 3 a lament? Why do you think there are so many lament psalms? What is David's specific sorrow here? What is the hope that he longs for? Is it easy for Christians to lament today? Why or why not?

More to Consider: Psalm 3 includes the first use of the word Selah *in Scripture (vv. 2, 4, 8). It is used seventy-one times in Psalms and three times in Habakkuk 3. It may come from the words meaning "to lift up" or "to be silent." Why might the psalmists have included this word in the psalms? How is it used today?*

From the Commentary

The morning was the most important time of the day for David, as it should be for us today.

It was in the morning that he met with the Lord and worshipped Him. It was his time to pray (5:3), to sing (57:7–8; 59:16), and to be satisfied by God's mercy (90:14).

—*Be Worshipful,* page 30

10. Why is the time of the day significant to David in this psalm? What is the symbolic relevance to Christians today? The practical relevance?

Looking Inward

Take a moment to reflect on all that you've explored thus far in this study of Psalms 1—3. Review your notes and answers and think about how each of these things matters in your life today.

Tips for Small Groups: To get the most out of this section, form pairs or trios and have group members take turns answering these questions. Be honest and as open as you can in this discussion, but most of all, be encouraging and supportive of others. Be sensitive to those who are going through particularly difficult times and don't press for people to speak if they're uncomfortable doing so.

11. Where do you turn to find wisdom today? What wisdom do you find from secular sources? How does it compare with what you find in Scripture? How does the wisdom you find in Scripture influence your practical living?

12. What are some of the ways you've rebelled against God (as the kings in Psalm 2 did)? Why did you rebel? What caused you to repent and turn to the Savior? What implications does all this have for how you relate to friends who are rebelling against God?

13. Describe a time when you felt the need to lament something. What did that lament look like? What model for lament does David give in Psalm 3 that you could apply to your own situation(s)?

Going Forward

14. Think of one or two things that you have learned that you'd like to work on in the coming week. Remember that this is all about quality, not quantity. It's better to work on one specific area of life and do it well than to work on many and do poorly (or to be so overwhelmed that you simply don't try).

Do you need to trust the wisdom in Scripture? Do you need to learn how to express your lament in a godly way? Be specific. Go back through Psalms 1—3 and put a star next to the phrase or verse that is most encouraging to you. Consider memorizing this verse.

Real-Life Application Ideas: If you've had a difficult circumstance in your life that continues to cause pain, why not write your own lament psalm like David did? Follow David's model and express your feelings honestly, along with your hope for resolution or reconciliation or even simple peace with the situation.

Seeking Help

15. Write a prayer below (or simply pray one in silence), inviting God to work on your mind and heart in those areas you've previously noted. Be honest about your desires and fears.

Notes for Small Groups:
- *Look for ways to put into practice the things you wrote in the Going Forward section. Talk with other group members about your ideas and commit to being accountable to one another.*
- *During the coming week, ask the Holy Spirit to continue to reveal truth to you from what you've read and studied.*
- *Before you start the next lesson, read Psalms 22—24. For more in-depth lesson preparation, read the related commentary in* Be Worshipful.

The Shepherd
(PSALMS 22—24)

Before you begin ...
- *Pray for the Holy Spirit to reveal truth and wisdom as you go through this lesson.*
- *Read Psalms 22—24. This lesson references content in* Be Worshipful. *It will be helpful for you to have your Bible and a copy of the commentary available as you work through this lesson.*

Getting Started

From the Commentary

Psalms 22; 23; and 24 form a trilogy on Christ the Shepherd. In 22, the Good Shepherd dies for the sheep (John 10:1–18); in 23, the Great Shepherd lives for the sheep and cares for them (Heb. 13:20–21); and in 24, the Chief Shepherd returns in glory to reward His sheep for their service (1 Peter 5:4).

David is the author of Psalm 22, but we have a difficult time finding an occasion in his life that would call forth this kind of psalm. According to the record, the Lord never deserted him in his hour of need but always provided friends to help him and deliverance from his enemies.

—*Be Worshipful*, page 90

1. What might have prompted David to write these three psalms? What is the mood in each of them? How would the imagery of the "Shepherd" have been received by the Israelites? How easy is it to relate to a shepherd in today's Christian culture?

More to Consider: The suffering David refers to in Psalm 22 is that of a criminal being executed. How do these psalms support the claim in Acts 2:30 that David was a prophet? How is his role as prophet different from the role of those we typically refer to as prophets?

2. Choose one verse or phrase from Psalms 22—24 that stands out to you. This could be something you're intrigued by, something that makes you

uncomfortable, something that puzzles you, something that resonates with you, or just something you want to examine further. Write that here.

Going Deeper

From the Commentary

> There were three burdens that moved David to pray for God's help, and they apply to Jesus as well.
>
> 1. He was abandoned by the Lord (22:1–5).
>
> 2. He was despised by the people (22:6–11).
>
> 3. He was condemned by the law (22:12–21).
> —*Be Worshipful,* pages 90–91

3. How are each of the burdens described above applicable to David? How are they applicable to Jesus? What other parallels can you see in Psalm 22 between David and Jesus?

From the Commentary

> With Psalm 22:22–31 we move now from suffering to glory, from prayer to praise (vv. 22, 23, 25, 26). In verses 1–21, Jesus "endured the cross," but now He enters into "the joy that was set before him" (Heb. 12:2; and see Jude v. 24). He had prayed to be delivered out of death (Heb. 5:7), and that prayer was answered.
>
> —*Be Worshipful,* pages 92–93

4. Go through Psalm 22 and circle phrases that are applicable to Jesus. How does the shift in emphasis from verses 1–21 to 22–31 relate to Jesus' story? What is the significance of 22:30–31 for today's church? What does a psalm like this one teach us about the greater plan God has for His people?

From Today's World

Psalm 23 is undoubtedly one of the best-known passages of Scripture among Christians, Jews, and even many who have no religious affiliation. It has been set to music countless times and is also a featured element in many other forms of media, including popular television shows and feature films. Perhaps known best for its frequent use at funerals, Psalm 23 has found a place in popular culture as a sort of touchstone for comfort in difficult times.

5. What do you think accounts for the popularity of this particular psalm? Why do you think it's especially popular for use in funeral ceremonies? What makes Psalm 23 more compelling to today's culture than other psalms? What comfort do people find in the words of this psalm?

From the Commentary

> Psalm 23 focuses on what Jesus does for us "all the days of [our] life" and not just at death (v. 6). It's also unfortunate that people tend to spiritualize the psalm and fail to see it in its true setting. They see David, a "young shepherd boy," lying on his back in the pasture and pondering the things of God, when he probably wrote this psalm late in life, possibly during the rebellion of his son Absalom (2 Sam. 13—19). In it, David deals with some of the difficult things he experienced during his long walk with the Lord.
>
> —*Be Worshipful*, page 94

6. How does the psalm take on a new meaning if David wrote it late in life? What are some of the unique ways this perspective can help people deal with difficult times? How does the psalm speak to the issues David dealt with around the time of his son's rebellion? What are some similar experiences in today's world where the psalm fits just as appropriately?

From the Commentary

> Psalm 23:4 is the central verse of the psalm, and the personal pronoun changes from *he* to *you*. David is not speaking *about* the shepherd but speaking *to* the shepherd. In the dark valley, He is not before us but beside us, leading the way and calming our fears.
>
> —*Be Worshipful,* page 96

7. How does the shift from *he* to *you* in verse 4 change the flavor and meaning of the psalm? Why is this important to the psalmist's message? How does this personalize the shepherd?

From the Commentary

Some students believe there is a change of metaphor in verse 5, from the shepherd and his sheep to the host and his guest, but this is not necessarily the case. "Table" doesn't necessarily refer to a piece of furniture used by humans, for the word simply means "something spread out." Flat places in the hilly country were called "tables," and sometimes the shepherd stopped the flock at these "tables" and allowed them to eat and rest as they headed for the fold (see Ps. 78:19). After each difficult day's work, the aim of the shepherd was to bring the flock safely back to the fold, where weary sheep could safely rest for the night.

—*Be Worshipful,* page 97

8. Does the meaning of the passage change if the "table" referred to in verse 5 refers to a host's dining table instead of a flat stretch of land? Why or why not? In what ways does verse 5 speak to believers today? What does it mean that the shepherd prepares a table "in the presence of my enemies"? Who are these enemies? What does it mean to be anointed with oil?

More to Consider: The rod referred to in this psalm was a heavy cudgel the shepherd could use to stun or kill attacking beasts. The staff would have likely been the shepherd's crook, which was used to assist the individual sheep. What symbolic purpose does each of these devices have for the "sheep" who are God's children?

From the Commentary

Most commentators connect Psalm 24 with David's bringing the ark of the covenant into Jerusalem (2 Sam. 6; 1 Chron. 15:1—16:3), and it may well be that David wrote it for that occasion. It appears to be an antiphonal psalm. The people (or a Levitical chorus) opened with verses 1–2; a leader asked the questions in verses 3, 8a, and 10a; and the chorus or the people answered with verses 4–6, 8b, and 10b. It was sung in Herod's temple each Sunday, and some connect the psalm with our Lord's entrance into Jerusalem on what we call Palm Sunday.

—*Be Worshipful,* page 98

9. How does this psalm take on unique significance by following the narrative of Psalm 23? What is the theme of this psalm? What three privileges does God give His people in this psalm? How is the shepherd presented in this psalm?

From the Commentary

> Five times in Psalm 24 God is called the King of Glory.
> Jesus is the Chief Shepherd who will one day return in
> glory and give each faithful servant a crown of glory (1
> Peter 5:1–4; and see Ps. 1:7; 4:11–14; 5:10; 1 Cor. 2:8). The
> gates of Jerusalem opened outward, so what is meant by
> "be lifted up"? Certainly there would be plenty of head-
> room for the Levites to carry in the ark, and it wouldn't
> be required to raise the lintels of the gates. Martin Luther
> translated it, "Open wide the portals," that is, "Give a
> hearty welcome to the Lord!"
>
> —*Be Worshipful,* page 100

10. Why is it significant that David refers to the "King of Glory" so many
times in Psalm 24? How does the regal flavor of this psalm compare and
contrast with the agrarian textures of Psalm 23?

Looking Inward

Take a moment to reflect on all that you've explored thus far in this study of Psalms 22—24. Review your notes and answers and think about how each of these things matters in your life today.

> *Tips for Small Groups: To get the most out of this section, form pairs or trios and have group members take turns answering these questions. Be honest and as open as you can in this discussion, but most of all, be encouraging and supportive of others. Be sensitive to those who are going through particularly difficult times and don't press for people to speak if they're uncomfortable doing so.*

11. When have you cried out like the psalmist in the first half of Psalm 22? What experiences in your life have led you to wonder if God was far from you? How did you work through those times? What "glory" did you experience on the other side of the suffering?

12. How has Psalm 23 been a comfort to you? What verses from that psalm have had the most influence on your seasons of suffering? How has your understanding of the psalm's meaning changed since you first heard it? What are some ways it applies to your life today?

13. What is your reaction to the grandeur and majesty of the praise in Psalm 24? In what ways do you see evidence that the world is the Lord's? How does this affect your daily life? What does it mean to you that God is the "King of Glory"?

Going Forward

14. Think of one or two things that you have learned that you'd like to work on in the coming week. Remember that this is all about quality, not quantity. It's better to work on one specific area of life and do it well than to work on many and do poorly (or to be so overwhelmed that you simply don't try).

Do you need to seek comfort in a difficult time? Do you want to better understand what it means that God is the King of Glory? Be specific. Go back through Psalms 22—24 and put a star next to the phrase or verse that is most encouraging to you. Consider memorizing this verse.

Real-Life Application Ideas: Think about ways you can be an extension of the Good Shepherd described in Psalm 23. What are some practical ways you can be a comfort to those who are suffering? Once you have some ideas, put them into action.

Seeking Help

15. Write a prayer below (or simply pray one in silence), inviting God to work on your mind and heart in those areas you've previously noted. Be honest about your desires and fears.

Notes for Small Groups:

- *Look for ways to put into practice the things you wrote in the Going Forward section. Talk with other group members about your ideas and commit to being accountable to one another.*

- *During the coming week, ask the Holy Spirit to continue to reveal truth to you from what you've read and studied.*

- *Before you start the next lesson, read Psalms 44—47. For more in-depth lesson preparation, read the related commentary in* Be Worshipful.

From Forsaken to Fortress
(PSALMS 44—47)

Before you begin ...
- *Pray for the Holy Spirit to reveal truth and wisdom as you go through this lesson.*
- *Read Psalms 44—47. This lesson references content in* Be Worshipful. *It will be helpful for you to have your Bible and a copy of the commentary available as you work through this lesson.*

Getting Started

From the Commentary

The Jewish people sang praises to God after their great victories (Ex. 15; Judg. 5), but Psalm 44 was sung after a humiliating defeat (vv. 9–14, 22). The parallels between Psalms 44 and 60 suggest that Edom and the Arameans were the enemies involved. (See 2 Sam. 8; 10; 1 Chron. 18.) Although Israel finally won great victories over their enemies, there must have been some defeats along the way that greatly disturbed the people.... Perhaps this psalm was used at a national "day of prayer" with a worship leader speaking the "I/my" verses and the people the "we/our" verses. The four stanzas that make up this psalm reveal four different attitudes on the part of the people.

—*Be Worshipful*, pages 164–65

1. How does Psalm 44 differ in tone and content from the others you've studied so far? In what ways would this psalm be a good reminder for the Israelites during difficult times? During good times? Why is it important to remember times of defeat as well as times of triumph?

2. Choose one verse or phrase from Psalms 44—47 that stands out to you. This could be something you're intrigued by, something that makes you uncomfortable, something that puzzles you, something that resonates with you, or just something you want to examine further. Write that here.

Going Deeper

From the Commentary

> Whenever there was trouble in Israel, the first explanation
> was usually "Somebody has sinned." Certainly this was
> true when Israel was defeated at Ai (Josh. 7), when there
> was a three-year famine in David's time (2 Sam. 21), and
> when David numbered the people (2 Sam. 24). But as far
> as the psalmist knew, there was no sin to be confessed
> because the people were faithful to the Lord.
>
> —*Be Worshipful*, pages 165–66

3. What does the uncertainty and confusion in this psalm tell us about the
way God chose to work in the lives of the Israelites during this chapter in
their story? How does the psalmist's pleading shift in verses 23–26? What
does this teach us about trusting God?

*More to Consider: Read Romans 8:28. How does this verse apply to
the events referred to in Psalm 44?*

From the Commentary

> Psalm 45 is a marriage song.... The wedding was obviously that of a king (vv. 1, 11, 14; and note the mention of throne, scepter, and majesty), and some have identified him with Solomon, who married an Egyptian princess (1 Kings 3:1; 9:24).... But it's clear that one "greater than Solomon" (Matt. 12:42) is present in this beautiful psalm, and that one is Jesus Christ, the King of Kings. If this were merely a secular love song, why would it be given to the chief musician to be used in the worship of the Lord at His sanctuary? That would be blasphemy.
>
> —*Be Worshipful*, page 167

4. What stands out to you about the descriptions in this psalm? Go through Psalm 45 and underline words or phrases that make it likely that this is a messianic psalm.

From the Commentary

> Psalm 45:7b–17 describes the royal wedding, beginning
> with *the preparation of the Bridegroom* (vv. 7b–9). The
> anointing in verse 7b is not His anointing as King but
> as the honored guest at the wedding feast. It is the "oil
> of gladness" representing the eternal joy that belongs to
> the happy bride and Bridegroom (Isa. 61:3). The soldiers
> gambled for our Lord's garments when He hung on the
> cross (John 19:23–24), but at the wedding feast, His gar-
> ments will be fragrant and glorious.
>
> —*Be Worshipful*, page 169

5. How does the description of the Bridegroom compare to our
understanding of Jesus as the Bridegroom for His bride, the church? What
is the "preparation of the bride" as described in Psalm 45:10–14? In what
ways is the church today being prepared for the Bridegroom?

From the History Books

Martin Luther's hymn "A Mighty Fortress Is Our God" was based on
Psalm 46. Luther composed both the words and melody between 1527 and

1529, and the hymn became popular in the early days of the Reformation, likely helping to draw support for the cause. This hymn was translated into many languages and remains popular in the United States today; it is not only used in church services but also referenced in television shows and movies, both for its theological content and, occasionally, to express irony.

6. What is it about this hymn that would have drawn supporters to the reformers' cause? What makes it relevant to today's church? Why might some in popular culture reference this particular hymn in an ironic context? What does this say about the meaning and importance of the message?

From the Commentary

The word translated "refuge" in Psalm 46:1 means "a shelter, a rock of refuge," while the word in verses 7 and 11 means "a stronghold, a high tower, a fortress." Both words declare that God is a dependable refuge for His people when everything around them seems to be falling apart.

—*Be Worshipful,* page 171

7. Why would the image of "refuge" have been important to the Israelites during the time of David? Why is that image important to the church today? What sorts of trouble do Christians experience today? What is the message in this psalm to those who are in trouble?

From the Commentary

"Be still" (v. 10) literally means "Take your hands off! Relax!" We like to be "hands-on" people and manage our own lives, but God is God, and we are but His servants. *Because Hezekiah and his leaders allowed God to be God, He delivered them from their enemies.* That was the way King Hezekiah had prayed: "Now therefore, O LORD our God, I pray, save us from his hand, that all the kingdoms of the earth may know that You are the LORD God, You alone" (2 Kings 19:19 NKJV). The Lord calls Himself "the God of Jacob," and we remember how often Jacob got into trouble because he got his hands on circumstances and tried to play God. There is a time to obey God and act, but until then, we had better take our hands off and allow Him to work in His own time and His own way.

—*Be Worshipful*, page 173

8. What does it mean to "Be still" today? Why is it difficult to trust God to manage our lives? What does allowing "God to be God" look like in practical terms? Why does God allow us to get into "tight places" in life? What do these experiences teach us about God?

From the Commentary

> The promise of Psalm 46:10 is fulfilled in Psalm 47, "I will be exalted among the nations, I will be exalted in the earth" (NASB). Five times the people are commanded to "sing praises" to the Lord, who "reigns over the nations" (v. 8 NASB). If Psalm 47 was written to celebrate the defeat of Sennacherib (see Ps. 46), then it describes the people of Israel proclaiming to the surrounding Gentile nations the glorious victory of their God, a victory won without their having to fight a battle!
>
> —*Be Worshipful,* page 174

9. In what ways is God exalted in Psalm 47? How is this a fulfillment of Psalm 46:10? What is the theme of Psalm 47? How is this theme appropriate to the culture of the Israelites? How does it apply today?

From the Commentary

> To know God is to know One who is awesome in all that
> He is, says, and does (65:8; 76:7, 12). Jerusalem's deliver-
> ance from Sennacherib proved once more that the God of
> Israel was greater than all gods and deserved all the praise
> His people could bring to Him. He gave them victory
> over the nations in Canaan and gave them the land for
> their inheritance.
>
> —*Be Worshipful,* page 174

10. What does Psalm 47 teach us about God's character? Why did the
Israelites praise God with such enthusiasm? What are ways churches today
praise God? Why is it important to offer praises to God?

Looking Inward

Take a moment to reflect on all that you've explored thus far in this study
of Psalms 44—47. Review your notes and answers and think about how
each of these things matters in your life today.

Tips for Small Groups: To get the most out of this section, form pairs or trios and have group members take turns answering these questions. Be honest and as open as you can in this discussion, but most of all, be encouraging and supportive of others. Be sensitive to those who are going through particularly difficult times and don't press for people to speak if they're uncomfortable doing so.

11. When have you felt like the psalmist in Psalm 44? What are the specific events that led you to wonder if God had forsaken you? Where was God during that season? How did God use that time to grow your faith? If you're still in one of those seasons, how can you trust that God is near?

12. How does the Bridegroom/bride analogy in Psalm 45 affect the way you view your relationship with Jesus? In what ways are you being prepared as part of the church for the wedding? Where do you see room for spiritual growth and improvement in your specific role in the church?

13. What does it mean to you that God is "a mighty fortress"? When has God been your refuge in a time of trouble? Psalm 46:2 says, "We will not fear," but is this a realistic claim? When have you experienced fear in difficult times? How has God come through in those times?

Going Forward

14. Think of one or two things that you have learned that you'd like to work on in the coming week. Remember that this is all about quality, not quantity. It's better to work on one specific area of life and do it well than to work on many and do poorly (or to be so overwhelmed that you simply don't try).

Do you need to learn to trust God when He seems to have forsaken you? Be specific. Go back through Psalms 44—47 and put a star next to the phrase or verse that is most encouraging to you. Consider memorizing this verse.

Real-Life Application Ideas: Ask your church to sing the hymn "A Mighty Fortress Is Our God" in an upcoming service. Or, if that's not feasible, simply get a CD with a rendition of the hymn and play it for your small group. Rather than turning the song into a study, simply enjoy the message and practice your own praise as it is sung.

Seeking Help

15. Write a prayer below (or simply pray one in silence), inviting God to work on your mind and heart in those areas you've previously noted. Be honest about your desires and fears.

Notes for Small Groups:

- *Look for ways to put into practice the things you wrote in the Going Forward section. Talk with other group members about your ideas and commit to being accountable to one another.*
- *During the coming week, ask the Holy Spirit to continue to reveal truth to you from what you've read and studied.*
- *Before you start the next lesson, read Psalms 65—68. For more in-depth lesson preparation, read the related commentary in* Be Worshipful.

God of Creation
(PSALMS 65—68)

Before you begin ...
- *Pray for the Holy Spirit to reveal truth and wisdom as you go through this lesson.*
- *Read Psalms 65—68. This lesson references content in Be Worshipful. It will be helpful for you to have your Bible and a copy of the commentary available as you work through this lesson.*

Getting Started

From the Commentary

Psalm 65 is the first of four psalms (65—68) that focus on praising the Lord for His manifold blessings in nature and for His gracious dealings with His people. He is the God of creation and the God of the covenant. Psalm 65 acknowledges our total dependence on the Lord to provide both our spiritual and material needs.

—Be Worshipful, page 210

1. Why is it important to praise God for His creation? How does the psalmist do this in Psalm 65? What does God's care of nature tell His people about His care for His followers?

More to Consider: The phrase "crown the year" (Ps. 65:11) suggests a harvest festival in October, the first month of Israel's civil year. How might previous experience with drought and famine—brought on by God Himself as discipline—have prompted this hopeful phrase?

2. Choose one verse or phrase from Psalms 65—68 that stands out to you. This could be something you're intrigued by, something that makes you uncomfortable, something that puzzles you, something that resonates with you, or just something you want to examine further. Write that here.

Going Deeper

From the Commentary

> The opening phrase in Psalm 65 is literally "To you praise is silence," which doesn't convey very much. The New American Standard Bible combines both: "There will be silence before You, and praise in Zion, O God." The Hebrew word for "silence" is very similar to the word for "fitting, proper," so some translate it, "Praise is fitting for you," that is, "It is fitting that your people praise you." But silence is also a part of worship, and we must learn to wait quietly before the Lord (62:1).
>
> —*Be Worshipful,* page 211

3. What strikes you about the tone of the opening verses in Psalm 65? What does the psalmist mean that "praise awaits you"? What does this tell us about the psalmist?

From the Commentary

> Psalm 65 opened in the tiny land of Israel (God's grace)
> and moved from there to the nations of the earth (God's
> government). Now in Psalm 65:9–13 the entire universe
> comes into the picture, for the Creator of the universe
> provides the sunshine and rain in their times and seasons
> so that people can plow the earth, plant seeds, and even-
> tually harvest food.
>
> —*Be Worshipful,* page 212

4. What does Psalm 65:5–8 tell us about God's role as ruler? What do verses
9–13 tell us about His role as provider? Why would these descriptions of
God have been particularly important to the small nation of Israel? In what
ways do they help underscore the chosenness of God's people? How do
they speak about God's relationship to the church today?

From the Commentary

> At the close of Psalm 65, you hear nature praising the
> Lord, and Psalm 66 exhorts all mankind to join creation

in celebrating God's greatness. It appears that Israel had gone through severe trials (vv. 8–12) and yet won a great victory with the Lord's help. Some students believe that this event was the Lord's miraculous defeat of Assyria (Isa. 36—37) and that the individual speaking in verses 13–20 was King Hezekiah, whose prayer the Lord answered (37:14–20). The exhortation to praise the Lord begins with the Gentile nations (vv. 1–7), moves to Israel (vv. 8–12), and concludes with the individual believer (vv. 13–20).

—*Be Worshipful*, page 213

5. If you didn't know the context in which Psalm 66 was written, what would stand out to you about the message? Review the defeat of Assyria in Isaiah 36—37. How does the meaning of this psalm change if verses 13–20 specifically refer to that event? What does a psalm like this teach us about how God's Word can speak to specific circumstances in history and also far beyond those events?

From the Commentary

> The change in Ps. 66:13–20 from "we/our" to "I/my" is significant, for corporate worship is the ministry of many individuals, and God sees each heart. During his times of trial, the psalmist had made vows to God, and now he hastened to fulfill them. He brought many burnt offerings to the altar, the very best he had, and they symbolized his total dedication to the Lord.
>
> —*Be Worshipful,* page 214

6. What would have prompted the psalmist to make vows to God, as referenced in Psalm 66:13–20? How does this kind of commitment to God compare and contrast to the way Christians commit to God today? How might the psalmist rewrite this psalm today, in light of Jesus' sacrifice on our behalf? What does the last verse (v. 20) tell the reader about prayer? Why is this important to the psalmist? To us today?

From the Commentary

> Except for verses 1 and 6, each verse in Psalm 67 men-
> tions "all nations" or "all peoples" and in that respect fits
> in with Psalms 65 and 66. It's a psalm of praise to God for
> all His blessings, as well as a prayer to God that His bless-
> ings will flow out to the Gentiles, especially His salvation.
>
> —*Be Worshipful,* page 215

7. Read Genesis 12:1–3. How does the message of Psalm 67 align with
God's covenant with Abraham? Whom is the psalmist asking God to
bless? What is the purpose of God's blessing?

From the Commentary

> What does the harvest (Ps. 67:6–7) have to do with the
> conversion of the nations of the world? The phrase "Then
> shall the earth yield her increase" (v. 6) is a quotation from
> Leviticus 26:4, and Leviticus 26 is a summary of God's
> covenant with Israel. (See also Deut. 28—30.) God made
> it clear that His blessing on the land depended on Israel's

obedience to His law (Lev. 26:1–13). The blessings He
would send Israel would be a witness to the pagan nations
that Jehovah alone is the true and living God, and this
would give the Jews the opportunity to share the Word
with them (Deut. 28:1–14). But if Israel disobeyed the
Lord, He would withhold the rain, and their fields would
yield no harvest (Lev. 26:14–39), and this would put
Israel to shame before the Gentile nations (Jer. 33:1–9;
Joel 2:17–19; Deut. 9:26–29).

—*Be Worshipful,* page 216

8. God's covenant with Israel associated blessing with obedience. After
reading some of the psalms, what can you tell about the effects of Israel's
obedience or lack thereof? How is this cause-effect illustrated in the words
of the psalms? How does Jesus' sacrifice redefine the relationship between
blessing and obedience?

*More to Consider: Read Judges 5 in preparation for studying Psalm
68. Note the comparisons between the two chapters. (For example: Ps.
68:4 and Judg. 5:3, 7–8).*

From the Commentary

> Psalm 68:1 is a quotation from Numbers 10:33–35, Israel's "marching cry" whenever they set out on their journeys. The quotation is fitting because the psalm pictures the Lord "on the march" on behalf of His people. He fights their battles, leads them into the land of their inheritance, and takes up residence in the sanctuary on Mount Zion.
>
> —*Be Worshipful,* page 217

9. How does David use Psalm 68 both as a record of history and as an encouragement to the Israelites? What is the significance of the phrase "father to the fatherless"? What does it mean that God "sets the lonely in families" and "leads forth the prisoners with singing"? How are these assurances applicable to the church today?

From the Commentary

> In Psalm 68:7–18, David reviewed the triumphant march of Israel, beginning with their exodus from Egypt and the journey to Sinai (vv. 7–8). The rain can be taken

literally, but it might also refer to the manna that came down six days a week (Ps. 78:24, 27; Ex. 16:4; Deut. 11:10–12). Then Israel entered the land and conquered it (Ps. 68:9–14) because the Lord spoke the Word of victory (v. 11; see 33:11). He had promised Israel they would take the land, and they did (Ex. 23:20–33; Deut. 11:22–32).

—*Be Worshipful,* page 217

10. Where in the psalm does the shift take place from "God is marching before us" to "God is dwelling with us"? Why was it important to acknowledge God's presence on Mt. Zion? In what ways might Psalm 68:28–35 be considered prophetic?

Looking Inward

Take a moment to reflect on all that you've explored thus far in this study of Psalms 65—68. Review your notes and answers and think about how each of these things matters in your life today.

Tips for Small Groups: To get the most out of this section, form pairs or trios and have group members take turns answering these questions.

Be honest and as open as you can in this discussion, but most of all, be encouraging and supportive of others. Be sensitive to those who are going through particularly difficult times and don't press for people to speak if they're uncomfortable doing so.

11. What does your praise for God look like? In what ways do you praise Him for His creation? Make a list of some good reasons to praise God for creation. What implications does this list have for how you go about your daily life?

12. What are some of the "battles" God has won for you? How have you shown your gratitude to Him for those victories? What are some of the battles you're currently facing? Is it easy to praise God in the middle of trials? Why or why not? What would it take for you to be able to praise God anyway?

13. In the Old Testament, God's covenant was all about obedience and blessing. In what ways do you live your life according to a similar belief? What are the dangers of believing we can earn God's blessings, in light of the sacrifice God made through His Son, Jesus? How do God's blessings rain down on Christians today?

Going Forward

14. Think of one or two things that you have learned that you'd like to work on in the coming week. Remember that this is all about quality, not quantity. It's better to work on one specific area of life and do it well than to work on many and do poorly (or to be so overwhelmed that you simply don't try).

Do you need to learn how to praise God for His creation? How to thank Him for the ways He has helped you through trials? Be specific. Go back through Psalms 65—68 and put a star next to the phrase or verse that is most encouraging to you. Consider memorizing this verse.

Real-Life Application Ideas: Take some time to focus on God's creation. Go for a walk. Visit a park or nature conservatory. Keep in mind that God's creation is more than nature—it's animals and people, too! During this focused time, record your praises in a journal.

Seeking Help

15. Write a prayer below (or simply pray one in silence), inviting God to work on your mind and heart in those areas you've previously noted. Be honest about your desires and fears.

Notes for Small Groups:

- *Look for ways to put into practice the things you wrote in the Going Forward section. Talk with other group members about your ideas and commit to being accountable to one another.*

- *During the coming week, ask the Holy Spirit to continue to reveal truth to you from what you've read and studied.*

- *Before you start the next lesson, read Psalms 73—75. For more in-depth lesson preparation, read the related commentary in* Be Worshipful.

⊞ Divine Worship
(PSALMS 73—75)

Before you begin ...
- *Pray for the Holy Spirit to reveal truth and wisdom as you go through this lesson.*
- *Read Psalms 73—75. This lesson references content in* Be Worshipful. *It will be helpful for you to have your Bible and a copy of the commentary available as you work through this lesson.*

Getting Started

From the Commentary

Asaph, Heman, and Ethan (Jeduthun) were Levites who served as musicians and worship leaders at the sanctuary during David's reign.... Apparently they established "guilds" for their sons and other musicians so they might carry on the worship traditions. Twelve psalms are attributed to Asaph (50; 73—83). Psalm 73 deals with the age-old problem of why the righteous suffer while the

ungodly seem to prosper (37; 49; Job 21; Jer. 12; Hab.
1:13ff.). Asaph could not lead the people in divine worship if he had questions about the ways of the Lord, but
he found in that worship the answer to his problems.

—*Be Worshipful,* page 235

1. How does the tone of Psalm 73 differ from those written by David?
What circumstances might have prompted Asaph to write, "I envied the
arrogant when I saw the prosperity of the wicked"? How is this sentiment
still valid today? Why do Christ-followers wrestle with this theme?

*More to Consider: The Hebrew word translated "but" in verses 2 and
28, and "yet" (nevertheless) in verse 23, indicates a sharp contrast.
How does this particular phrasing suggest a difference between
"doubt" and "unbelief"?*

2. Choose one verse or phrase from Psalms 73—75 that stands out to you.
This could be something you're intrigued by, something that makes you
uncomfortable, something that puzzles you, something that resonates with
you, or just something you want to examine further. Write that here.

Going Deeper

From the Commentary

> From Asaph's viewpoint, the ungodly had it made. They
> were healthy (Ps. 73:4–5) and had no struggles in either
> life or death (Job 21:13, 23). They were proud of their
> wealth and stations in life, and they wore that pride like
> jewelry. They used violence to get their wealth and wore
> that violence like rich garments.
>
> —*Be Worshipful,* page 236

3. Circle the descriptions Asaph uses to portray the ungodly in Psalm 73.
What makes this psalm more than simply "complaining" about others'
success? What does it say about the relationship between wealth and God's
chosen people? How is this lesson applicable today?

From the Commentary

> Based on the evidence he could see around him, Asaph
> came to the wrong conclusion that he has wasted his time

and energy maintaining clean hands and a pure heart
(Ps. 73:1, 13; and see 24:4; 26:6). If he had ever read the
book of Job, then he had missed its message, for we don't
serve God because of what we get out of it but because *He
is worthy of our worship and service regardless of what He
allows to come to our lives.*

—*Be Worshipful,* pages 236–37

4. Why do you think Asaph missed the point in his understanding of
what it meant to serve God (Ps. 73:13–14)? How do people miss that
point today? Why is it such an easy mistake to make? What is the proper
response to God when a person sees the success of others while that person
is in the midst of trials?

From Today's World

Some Christians today are very successful and have everything they could
ever want and need, materially and otherwise. Or at least that's how it
appears. Their material success still stands in sharp contrast to a large
majority of believers who live from check to check or don't have enough
money to stay afloat at all. While some of these rich Christians are very

generous with their wealth, others might be rightly attacked for living a flamboyant lifestyle that flaunts their wealth.

5. What is it about wealth that divides believers so quickly and dramatically? Why do some Christians hold tight to the idea that wealth comes to those who truly believe? How is this similar to the struggle the psalmist has in Psalm 73? Why is it easy to fall into the trap that says obedience to God should result in greater wealth or worldly success?

From the Commentary

When the worship service ended and Asaph had gotten his feet firmly grounded on the faith, he left the sanctuary and told everybody what he had learned. He had drawn near to God, he had trusted God, and now he was ready to declare God's works. "Yet in all these things we are more than conquerors through Him who loved us" (Rom. 8:37 NKJV).

—*Be Worshipful,* page 238

6. What lessons can we glean from Psalm 73 to help us better respond to those who have apparent success and wealth in contrast to those who are suffering? What concluding truth does Psalm 73:26–28 offer to the discussion about what's truly important? How is this lived out in daily life?

From the Commentary

> Psalm 73 deals with a personal crisis of faith, but Psalm 74 moves to the national scene and focuses on the destruction of the temple in Jerusalem by the Babylonians in 587–86 BC. The author is obviously not the Asaph of David's day but a namesake among his descendants. Psalm 79 is a companion psalm, and you will find parallel passages in the book of Lamentations and Jeremiah. Even though the prophets had warned that judgment was coming (2 Chron. 36:15–21), the fall of Jerusalem and the destruction of the temple were catastrophic events that shook the people's faith.
>
> *—Be Worshipful,* page 238

7. How does the psalmist's tone shift from despair to confidence in Psalm 74? What are modern parallels to the despair the psalmist felt after the destruction of the temple? What does this psalm teach us about God's willingness to embrace our pain? About the ultimate answer to that pain?

From the Commentary

> Verse 12 is the central verse of Psalm 74 and the turning point in Asaph's experience. He lifted his eyes by faith from the burning ruins to the holy throne of God in the heavens and received a new perspective on the situation. (The Asaph who wrote Psalm 73 had a similar experience; see 73:17.)
>
> —*Be Worshipful*, page 240

8. What does Psalm 74:12 tell us about Asaph's understanding of God's role in the midst of his despair? How does he count upon past experiences with God to support his trust in God's presence and Lordship? Why does the psalmist come to the conclusion that the Lord remembers His people (vv. 18–23)? What role does tradition—God's noted role in historical events—play in our understanding of God and His ways today?

More to Consider: Though the Babylonians destroyed the temple, they did not destroy the God of the temple, Jehovah. What does this truth teach us today about where God resides? What practical implications does it have for today's churches?

From the Commentary

True worship centers on the Lord and not on us, our personal problems, or "felt needs." We praise God for who He is—His glorious attributes—and for His wonderful works (see Ps. 44:1–8; 77:12; 107:8, 15). God's name is a synonym for God's person and presence (Deut. 4:7; Isa. 30:27). He is indeed "a very present help in trouble" (Ps. 46:1), and when God's people call on the Lord, they know He will hear them.

—*Be Worshipful,* page 241–42

9. What does the psalmist mean by the phrase "your Name is near" in Psalm 75:1? How does the psalmist define God's character in this psalm? What is significant about the way the psalmist "quotes" God in this psalm? How does this help to turn the focus to who God is, rather than the problems we take to God?

From the Commentary

> If we expect the Lord to receive our words of praise, we
> must pay attention to His Word of truth as it is read, sung,
> and preached. The message delivered in Psalm 75:2–5 was
> twofold: a word of encouragement for believers (vv. 2–3)
> and a word of warning to the godless (vv. 4–5).
>
> —*Be Worshipful,* page 242

10. Why does the psalmist address two different audiences in this psalm? This seems to be a common thread. Is this also true of today's church? What are some ways the church reaches out to both believers and the ungodly? Read Psalm 75:9. What does the psalmist's personalization of the message teach us about what our worship ought to entail?

Looking Inward

Take a moment to reflect on all that you've explored thus far in this study of Psalms 73—75. Review your notes and answers and think about how each of these things matters in your life today.

Tips for Small Groups: To get the most out of this section, form pairs or trios and have group members take turns answering these questions. Be honest and as open as you can in this discussion, but most of all, be encouraging and supportive of others. Be sensitive to those who are going through particularly difficult times and don't press for people to speak if they're uncomfortable doing so.

11. Have you ever been frustrated by the way bad people are prosperous while good people struggle? Explain. What does this frustration say about your view of God's blessing? What greater truth can help you deal with the reality that sometimes good things happen to apparently undeserving people?

12. Is it important to you to maintain clean hands and a pure heart? Why or why not? What is a proper motivation for doing this? What is a wrong-minded motive? How does the message in Psalm 73 help you find proper perspective on blessing and the reasons to maintain a pure heart?

13. When have you felt like the psalmist in Psalm 74? What circumstances have led to feelings of despair? How have you found your way through those times? What does it take to lift your eyes to God's throne when you're struggling with difficult times? What are practical things you can do to move from despair to confidence in God?

Going Forward

14. Think of one or two things that you have learned that you'd like to work on in the coming week. Remember that this is all about quality, not quantity. It's better to work on one specific area of life and do it well than to work on many and do poorly (or to be so overwhelmed that you simply don't try).

Do you need to learn to trust God when you feel you're being treated unfairly? Do you need to grow confidence in God's nearness for difficult times? Be specific. Go back through Psalms 73—75 and put a star next to the phrase or verse that is most encouraging to you. Consider memorizing this verse.

> *Real-Life Application Ideas: Take inventory of the many blessings you have in your life. Don't focus primarily on material things but rather on the things that matter to God: faith, family, joy, hope, etc. Memorize this list and refer to it often as a reminder of God's goodness and as a prompt to worship God.*

Seeking Help

15. Write a prayer below (or simply pray one in silence), inviting God to work on your mind and heart in those areas you've previously noted. Be honest about your desires and fears.

Notes for Small Groups:

- *Look for ways to put into practice the things you wrote in the Going Forward section. Talk with other group members about your ideas and commit to being accountable to one another.*
- *During the coming week, ask the Holy Spirit to continue to reveal truth to you from what you've read and studied.*
- *Before you start the next lesson, read Psalms 85—88. For more in-depth lesson preparation, read the related commentary in* Be Worshipful.

Restoration, Character, and Suffering

(PSALMS 85—88)

Before you begin ...

- *Pray for the Holy Spirit to reveal truth and wisdom as you go through this lesson.*
- *Read Psalms 85—88. This lesson references content in* Be Worshipful. *It will be helpful for you to have your Bible and a copy of the commentary available as you work through this lesson.*

Getting Started

From the Commentary

Psalm 85 was probably written after the Jewish people returned to their land following their seventy years of captivity in Babylon (Jer. 29). Note the emphasis on *the land* (Ps. 85:1, 9, and 12) and on God's anger against His people (vv. 3–5). God gave them favor with their captors, raised up leaders like Zerubbabel the governor, Joshua the

high priest, and Ezra the scribe, and protected the Jewish
remnant as they traveled to their war-ravaged land.

—*Be Worshipful,* page 268

1. What prompts the psalmist to ask God for restoration in Psalm 85:4?
If God has just returned the Israelites to their land after a long season of
captivity, how might this have contributed to the plea? What would have
led the psalmist to ask, "Will you be angry with us forever" (v. 5)?

*More to Consider: Scottish preacher George H. Morrison said, "The
victorious Christian life is a series of new beginnings." How does this
message apply to the psalmist's words in Psalm 85? How does it apply
to us today?*

2. Choose one verse or phrase from Psalms 85—88 that stands out to you.
This could be something you're intrigued by, something that makes you
uncomfortable, something that puzzles you, something that resonates with
you, or just something you want to examine further. Write that here.

Going Deeper

From the Commentary

> It is one thing for the nation collectively to have a new birth
> of freedom, but there must also be changes in individuals.
> The praise begun in Psalm 85:1–3 (possibly by a choir) now
> becomes prayer from the hearts of the people in verse 4.
> Note that the word *us* is used six times, for it is the people
> who are praying, not the choir or worship leader.
>
> —*Be Worshipful*, page 269

3. What does Psalm 85 teach us about the importance and role of corporate worship? How does it also illustrate the role of individual worship? How do the two work together in the life of the believer?

From the Commentary

> In Psalm 85:10–13, the Lord announced future blessings
> that He would send if His people continued to walk with
> Him. Righteousness and peace—attributes of God—are

personified and would "kiss" each other, for the warfare would be over. (See Isa. 32:17; Rom. 3:21–31; 5:1–3.)

—*Be Worshipful,* page 270

4. How might Psalm 85:10–13 reveal a glimpse of the coming Christ? What does it mean that "righteousness and peace kiss each other"? What does the phrase "faithfulness springs forth from the earth" refer to?

From the Commentary

In the midst of a group of four psalms attributed to the sons of Korah, you find one psalm by David, Psalm 86, the only Davidic psalm in the entire third book of Psalms. When David wrote it, he was facing some formidable enemies whom we cannot identify (v. 14), at a time when he was "poor and needy" (v. 1) and calling for God's help. The remarkable thing about the psalm is that it is a mosaic of quotations from other parts of the Old Testament, especially from Psalms 25—28; 40; and 54—57; and Exodus 34. Since David wrote these psalms, he had every right to quote from them and adapt them to his present needs.

—*Be Worshipful,* page 271

5. What does the manner in which Psalm 86 was written (collected quotations from other chapters) say about its author? About the circumstances that prompted David to write this? How is this approach similar to the way Christians today find encouragement in others' writings?

From the Commentary

"There is none like unto thee!" (Ps. 86:8) is the confession of a man who truly knows God and remembered Israel's confession at the exodus (Ex. 15:11). During ten years of exile in the wilderness of Judea, David had learned much about God's character and the way He works in the lives of His people.

—*Be Worshipful,* page 272

6. Circle phases or words that describe God's character in Psalm 86. When do we learn most about God's character? What wisdom about God's character do you find in this psalm?

From the Commentary

> Psalm 87 must be read on two levels. It is a prophecy of the future kingdom, when all nations will come to Jerusalem to worship (Ps. 86:9; Isa. 2:1–5), and it is also a picture of the heavenly Zion where the children of God have their spiritual citizenship (Luke 10:20; Gal. 4:21–31; Phil. 3:20–21; Heb. 12:18–24). God promised that Abraham would have an earthly family, like the sands of the sea, which is Israel, and a heavenly family, like the stars of the heaven, which is the church (Gen. 13:16; 15:4–5).
>
> —*Be Worshipful*, page 273

7. Read the related Scripture passages in the previous commentary excerpt. How do these help to shed light on the meaning of Psalm 87? What does this teach us about the intricate nature of God's plan for His people?

From the Commentary

> Psalm 88 speaks of darkness, life in the depths, the immanence of death, feelings of drowning, loneliness, and imprisonment. The author, Heman, was a servant of God who was suffering intensely and did not understand why, yet he persisted in praying to God and did not abandon his faith.
>
> —*Be Worshipful,* page 276

8. Go through Psalm 88 and circle the references to suffering. What does this tell you about the psalmist's circumstances? Why is it important for the book of Psalms to include darker psalms like this one? What does this tell us about the importance of freely expressing despair to God?

More to Consider: Read Psalm 88:2; then 18:6; 22:24; 35:13; 66:20; 79:11. What do these verses teach us about prayer?

From Today's World

In a world where suffering is prevalent—not only on a global scale with war and natural disasters, but also on a very personal level with an apparent rise in emotional and psychological disorders—the search for answers has led to a rapid rise in books offering solutions to the problem of pain. They range from books offering blatant answers in the form of some "secret" to getting what you want, to diet books proclaiming the answer is all about what we eat. While there may be some truth in each of these, few books outside of those written by Christians pointing to Scripture have more than temporary or incomplete solutions.

9. Why do people seek quick fixes to pain? What does secular culture offer as an answer to pain? Why will this always come up short without the healing truth of God's Word?

From the Commentary

We do not know what this affliction was that came to the psalmist early in life, but it is painful to think that he suffered all his life long and all day long (Ps. 88:15, 17). He could not even look back to a time in his life when he enjoyed good health. The billows that had almost drowned him (v. 7) now became the fiery waves of torment (v. 16) as God's "burning anger" went over him (see Ps. 42:7). The flood was rising, and he felt he was about to drown (see 130:1), and there was nobody near enough to rescue him. He was alone!

—Be Worshipful, page 278

10. Read Job 13:15. How does this verse apply to the psalmist's situation in Psalm 88? What does it tell us that the psalmist, even though he is suffering, is still reaching out to God for an answer? What does this psalm say about the role of questions, and even of complaints, in the Christian life?

Looking Inward

Take a moment to reflect on all that you've explored thus far in this study of Psalms 85—88. Review your notes and answers and think about how each of these things matters in your life today.

Tips for Small Groups: To get the most out of this section, form pairs or trios and have group members take turns answering these questions.

Be honest and as open as you can in this discussion, but most of all, be encouraging and supportive of others. Be sensitive to those who are going through particularly difficult times and don't press for people to speak if they're uncomfortable doing so.

11. Describe a season in life when you longed for restoration. What led up to that desire? Have you ever felt like God was angry with you? What did you do with this feeling? What are the steps you need to take to find restoration and resolution?

12. Describe a time when you were "poor and needy" as David was when he wrote Psalm 86. What sources of comfort and encouragement did you draw from to move toward a place of peace?

13. If you've ever felt like the author of Psalm 88, what prompted that feeling? How do you deal with seasons of suffering? How do you deal with the suffering of those close to you? How can you keep pursuing God like the psalmist—in practical ways—when you're experiencing suffering?

Going Forward

14. Think of one or two things that you have learned that you'd like to work on in the coming week. Remember that this is all about quality, not quantity. It's better to work on one specific area of life and do it well than to work on many and do poorly (or to be so overwhelmed that you simply don't try).

Do you need to trust God in the midst of suffering? Do you want to discover how to better worship both individually and corporately? Be specific. Go back through Psalms 85—88 and put a star next to the phrase or verse that is most encouraging to you. Consider memorizing this verse.

Real-Life Application Ideas: Suffering is a familiar theme in the psalms, but so is worship and praise. Take time to pray this week for those you know (and those you don't) who are suffering from various circumstances. If you're suffering right now, ask a close friend or family member to join you and include your situation in a time of prayer.

Seeking Help

15. Write a prayer below (or simply pray one in silence), inviting God to work on your mind and heart in those areas you've previously noted. Be honest about your desires and fears.

Notes for Small Groups:
- *Look for ways to put into practice the things you wrote in the Going Forward section. Talk with other group members about your ideas and commit to being accountable to one another.*
- *During the coming week, ask the Holy Spirit to continue to reveal truth to you from what you've read and studied.*
- *Before you start the next lesson, read Psalms 93; 95—100. For more in-depth lesson preparation, read the related commentary in* Be Exultant.

Magnifying the King

(PSALMS 93; 95—100)

Before you begin ...
- *Pray for the Holy Spirit to reveal truth and wisdom as you go through this lesson.*
- *Read Psalms 93; 95—100. This lesson references content in* Be Exultant. *It will be helpful for you to have your Bible and a copy of the commentary available as you work through this lesson.*

Getting Started

From the Commentary

Psalms 93 and 95—100 emphasize the sovereign rule of Jehovah, the King of Israel, in the affairs of the nations.... Psalm 93 was perhaps written by one of the Levites who returned to Judah with the Jewish remnant after the Babylonian captivity.... It was an especially difficult time for the Jewish remnant (see Ezra and Haggai), and their work was interrupted, attacked, and neglected. The leaders and the people needed encouragement to continue the work, and this encouragement could come only from the Lord.

—*Be Exultant,* page 30

1. How might Psalm 93 have encouraged the Israelites? What does this psalm tell us about God's character? Why was this important for the Israelites during their season of challenges and trials? How can this psalm uplift Christians today?

More to Consider: The raging seas and pounding waves (Ps. 93:3–4) are often used as symbols for the rise and fall of a nation. (See also Ps. 46:1–3, 6; 65:6–7; 74:13–14; Isa. 17:12–13; Dan. 7:1–3; Luke 21:25; Rev. 13:1; 17:15.) Why do you think this imagery is appropriate?

2. Choose one verse or phrase from Psalms 93; 95—100 that stands out to you. This could be something you're intrigued by, something that makes you uncomfortable, something that puzzles you, something that resonates with you, or just something you want to examine further. Write that here.

Going Deeper

From the Commentary

> When the tempest is around us, we look by faith to the
> throne of grace above us and the Word of God before us.
> The truth about what is going on in this world is not in
> the newspapers but in the Scriptures. The false prophets
> among the Jews in Babylon gave a message different from
> that of Jeremiah, the true prophet of the Lord (Jer. 29),
> but it was the messages of God's servants that finally
> proved true.... False prophets, false teachers, and scoffers
> abound (2 Peter 2—3), but God's promises will all be ful-
> filled in their time, and God's children live by promises,
> not explanations.
>
> *—Be Exultant,* pages 31–32

3. Respond to the statement "The truth about what is going on in this
world is not in the newspapers but in the Scriptures." How is this borne
out in Psalm 93? In what ways does this psalm underscore the truth that
God always keeps His word?

From the Commentary

> Praise means looking up, but worship means bowing down. Alas, some people who enjoy lifting their hands and shouting do not enjoy bowing their knees and submitting. True worship is much deeper than communal praise, for worship involves realizing the awesomeness of God and experiencing the fear of the Lord and a deeper love for Him.
>
> —*Be Exultant,* page 36

4. Read Psalm 95. How does this psalm express praise? In what ways does it invoke worship? What does it mean to bow down before God? What does this look like in daily living? How can our daily living be a form of worship?

From Today's World

In many of today's churches, hymn singing has been supplanted by a more diverse time of praise and worship music. While not a universal truth, it is probably fair to say that praise music is more often about looking up, whereas hymns, rooted in deep theology, are more often about bowing down. For some, the time of praise and worship is a very personal time, though often experienced in a corporate setting. For some believers, the worship music is so important that they make their decision on which church to attend based solely on their experience of it.

5. Why have hymns lost their appeal to many churchgoers? What is it about the praise and worship time in a church that makes it so important to congregants? In what ways do the psalms give us good guidelines for praise? For worship? What are the dangers of basing your church attendance on the praise and worship time? What are the benefits?

From the Commentary

> In Psalm 96:1–3, we are commanded three times to sing to the Lord, and this parallels the three times in verses 7–8 that the psalmist commands us to "give" ("ascribe," NASB, NIV) glory to Him. (For "a new song," see Ps. 33:3.) A new experience of God's blessing, a new truth discovered in the Word, a new beginning after a crisis, a new open door for service—all of these can make an old song new or give us a new song from the Lord.
>
> —*Be Exultant,* pages 38–39

6. What does it look like to "ascribe" glory to God? What are some of the things that likely inspired the "new song" for the psalmist? What are some of the things that inspire "new songs" today?

From the Commentary

> No matter what the circumstances around us or the feelings within us, "the Lord reigns" (Ps. 93:1; 96:10; 99:1; 117:1), and He reigns over all the earth (Ps. 97:1, 4, 5, 9; 96:1, 9, 11, 13; 98:3, 4, 9). His sovereign authority reaches beyond the land of Israel to the farthest islands and coastlands, places that the Jews had never visited.
>
> —*Be Exultant,* page 40

7. Why was it important for the psalmist in Psalm 97 to invite the whole earth to be glad? What would the "distant shores" have represented to the Israelites? What are the "distant shores" for us today? Is it always easy to accept that "the Lord reigns" when circumstances are difficult? Why or why not? How does this psalm address that challenge?

From the Commentary

> From Psalm 98 Isaac Watts found the inspiration for his
> popular hymn "Joy to the World," often classified as a
> Christmas carol but more accurately identified as a "king-
> dom hymn." Watts described Christ's *second* advent and
> not His first, the messianic kingdom and not the manger.
> The parallels to Psalm 96 are obvious, but the psalms are
> not identical. Psalm 98 was written to praise the Lord for
> a great victory over Israel's enemies.
>
> —*Be Exultant,* page 43

8. What is your emotional response to Psalm 98? What does the tone of
this psalm tell you about the psalmist? About the Israelites' relationship to
God during this period of their history? What are the clues that this is a
messianic psalm?

More to Consider: Read Romans 8:18–25 and Revelation 22:20.
How might these passages relate to the theme in Psalm 98:7–9?

From the Commentary

> You could not approach the throne of the king of Persia
> unless he held out his scepter and gave you permission
> (Est. 4:10–11), but access to God's throne is available to
> His children through Jesus Christ (Heb. 10:19–25). Under
> the old covenant, God provided priests who ministered at
> the altar and were mediators between His needy people
> and their Lord, but today Jesus Christ is the Mediator
> (1 Tim. 2:5) who constantly intercedes for us (Rom. 8:34;
> Heb. 7:25). To the lost sinner, God's throne is a throne of
> judgment, but to the believer, it is a throne of grace (Heb.
> 4:14–16), and we can come to Him with our worship and
> praise as well as our burdens and needs.
>
> —*Be Exultant,* pages 45–46

9. Read Psalm 99. How does this psalm portray the royalty of the Lord?
Why was it important for the Israelites to see the Lord as their king? In
what ways does the church today honor the Lord's kingship?

From the Commentary

> For centuries, Christian congregations have sung
> William Kethe's paraphrase of Psalm 100, wedded to the
> beloved tune "Old Hundredth." First published in 1561,
> the words summarize the message of the psalm and help
> the worshippers give thanks to the Lord. Sometimes the
> traditional "Doxology" ("Praise God, from whom all
> blessings flow") by Thomas Ken is sung as the last verse.
>
> —*Be Exultant,* page 46

10. In what ways is Psalm 100 a fitting climax to the collection of "royal psalms" (93; 95—100)? What is the underlying message of this (and of all the royal psalms)? What does this psalm say to individuals about entering worship? In what ways can it help direct the corporate worship in today's churches?

Looking Inward

Take a moment to reflect on all that you've explored thus far in this study of Psalms 93; 95—100. Review your notes and answers and think about how each of these things matters in your life today.

Tips for Small Groups: To get the most out of this section, form pairs or trios and have group members take turns answering these questions. Be honest and as open as you can in this discussion, but most of all, be encouraging and supportive of others. Be sensitive to those who are going through particularly difficult times and don't press for people to speak if they're uncomfortable doing so.

11. When have you been encouraged by a psalm or song while going through a difficult time? How can encouraging words offer help and healing? What do you learn about God through the words offered in praise and worship?

12. The psalms teach us that God always keeps His word. How has this been true in your experience? Are there circumstances where you wrestle with doubt about this truth? Explain. How can the psalms help to allay those doubts and fears?

13. What does treating God as King involve for you? What are the challenges of having a King over you? What are the benefits? What are the things in your heart that draw you toward God as King? What are the things that move you to resist God's kingship?

Going Forward

14. Think of one or two things that you have learned that you'd like to work on in the coming week. Remember that this is all about quality, not quantity. It's better to work on one specific area of life and do it well than to work on many and do poorly (or to be so overwhelmed that you simply don't try).

Do you want to learn how to worship better? Do you need to treat God as King in some way? Be specific. Go back through Psalms 93; 95—100 and put a star next to the phrase or verse that is most encouraging to you. Consider memorizing this verse.

> *Real-Life Application Ideas: Plan or simply attend a praise and worship service specifically dedicated to a diversity of music—some that is "looking up" in praise, and some that is about "bowing down" in worship. As you experience both of these, listen for God's truth to speak through the music and the words.*

Seeking Help

15. Write a prayer below (or simply pray one in silence), inviting God to work on your mind and heart in those areas you've previously noted. Be honest about your desires and fears.

Notes for Small Groups:

- *Look for ways to put into practice the things you wrote in the Going Forward section. Talk with other group members about your ideas and commit to being accountable to one another.*

- *During the coming week, ask the Holy Spirit to continue to reveal truth to you from what you've read and studied.*

- *Before you start the next lesson, read Psalms 102—105. For more in-depth lesson preparation, read the related commentary in* Be Exultant.

The Creator and His Nation

(PSALMS 102—105)

Before you begin …
- *Pray for the Holy Spirit to reveal truth and wisdom as you go through this lesson.*
- *Read Psalms 102—105. This lesson references content in* Be Exultant. *It will be helpful for you to have your Bible and a copy of the commentary available as you work through this lesson.*

Getting Started

From the Commentary

Psalm 102 is both a penitential psalm and a messianic psalm. The anonymous author probably wrote it long after the destruction of Jerusalem, about the time he thought Jeremiah's prophecy of the seventy-year captivity was about to be fulfilled.

The longer we live, the more evidence we see that *things*

will change.... There are the normal changes of life, from birth to maturity to death, but there are also providential changes that God sends for our good and His glory. Many Jewish leaders in the days of Jeremiah the prophet thought that God would never allow Judah to be captured and Jerusalem and the temple destroyed (Jer. 7), but the Babylonian army did all three.

—*Be Exultant,* pages 51–52

1. Circle phrases in Psalm 102 that suggest the psalmist is perplexed or bothered by circumstances. How is the psalmist's response to uncertainty similar to things Christians experience today? What are some examples of situations when believers wonder if God has turned His face from them? What is this psalm's answer to that anxiety?

2. Choose one verse or phrase from Psalms 102—105 that stands out to you. This could be something you're intrigued by, something that makes you uncomfortable, something that puzzles you, something that resonates with you, or just something you want to examine further. Write that here.

Going Deeper

From the Commentary

> The psalmist was afraid he would die in midlife and never
> see the restoration of Judah, Jerusalem, and the temple.
> (See Isa. 38:10.) The eternal God would remain forever,
> but frail humans have only a brief time on earth (Ps.
> 90:1–12). Psalm 102:25–27 is quoted in Hebrews 1:10–12
> and applied to Jesus Christ, which reminds us that it is in
> Him that these promises will be fulfilled.
>
> *—Be Exultant,* page 54

3. What prompts the psalmist's urgency in Psalm 102? What does the contrast of the psalmist's fear (Psalm 102:11) and God's enduring nature (v. 27) teach us about the importance of trusting God?

More to Consider: Read Psalm 102:28. What practical implications does this final line in the psalm have for Christians today?

From the Commentary

> To "bless the Lord" (Ps. 103:1–6) means to delight His
> heart by expressing love and gratitude for all He is and all
> He does. Parents are pleased when their children simply
> thank them and love them, without asking for anything.
> True praise comes from a grateful heart that sincerely
> wants to glorify and please the Lord. "All that is within
> me" means that all of our inner beings are focused on the
> Lord—heart, soul, mind, and strength (Mark 12:28–31).
> It also means that we are prepared to obey His will after
> our praise has ended.
>
> —*Be Exultant,* pages 54–55

4. What are some examples of "true praise" in modern church culture?
(Not just the praise and worship time during the service.) What are ways
people praise God today outside of the corporate setting? What are some of
the distractions that make it difficult to praise with all your inmost being?

From the Commentary

> The nation of Israel was certainly blessed of the Lord and
> therefore obligated to express their praise and thanksgiv-
> ing to Him. Jehovah was their righteous Deliverer (v. 6),
> not only when He rescued them from Egypt, but also all
> during their history.
>
> *—Be Exultant,* page 56

5. In what ways does Psalm 103 reflect Israel's history with God as a nation?
What would you add to the psalm to reflect the church's history with God?
How does remembering our shared history affect the way Christians praise
God?

From the Commentary

> Psalm 104 opens with the description of a King so great
> (Ps. 95:3; Hab. 3:4) that He wears light for a robe (Ps.
> 93:1; Isa. 59:17; 1 John 1:5; 1 Tim. 6:16) and has a palace
> in heaven above the waters (Gen. 1:7). He uses the clouds
> for His chariot and the winds to move them (Ps. 18:7–15;

68:4; 77:16–19). His servants (the angels, 148:8; Heb 1:7) serve as quickly and invisibly as the wind and possess awesome power like flames of fire.

—Be Exultant, page 59

6. How does Psalm 104 reflect the content of Genesis 1? What attitudes does this psalm suggest God has toward the nonhuman parts of His creation? Why is it important to recognize the Creator's glory? How can the church do this today?

From Today's World

Our culture's interest in the "green" phenomenon has turned environmental responsibility into something akin to a religion for some. Every industry is being challenged to rethink its operations to be more earth-friendly. This has many positive benefits, but it has also become a touch point for much political positioning and debate.

7. Why is the environment such a controversial topic? How does the truth of God's role as Creator intersect with the conversation about the environment? How does praise for God's creation translate into care for His creation?

From the Commentary

> Whether we study invisible microscopic life, visible plant
> and animal life, human life, or the myriad of things that
> have no life, the diversity in creation is amazing. God could
> have made a drab, colorless world, one season everywhere,
> only one variety of each plant and animal, cookie-cutter
> humans, no musical sounds, and a few minimal kinds of
> food—but He did not, and how grateful we are! Only a
> wise God could have planned so many different things,
> and only a powerful God could have brought them into
> being.
>
> *—Be Exultant,* page 60

8. How does Psalm 104:24–35 demonstrate the wisdom and creativity of
our God? What does it say about God that He chose to create such a
diverse world? What does it say about us?

*More to Consider: Read 1 Timothy 6:17. How does this verse speak to
our stewardship role toward the earth?*

From the Commentary

> Psalm 105 focuses on the God of the covenant (vv. 8–10)
> who works out His divine purposes in human history.
> "Make known his deeds" (vv. 1–2, 5) is the major thrust,
> referring, of course, to God's mighty acts on behalf of
> Israel. (See also 78, and note that 105:1–15 is adapted
> in 1 Chron. 16:8–22.) The psalm does not go beyond
> the conquest of Canaan (v. 44) or mention the Davidic
> dynasty, which suggests that it may have been written
> after the Babylonian exile, possibly by one of the Levites
> who returned to Judah with the Jewish remnant.
>
> —*Be Exultant*, page 61

9. How does Psalm 105 combine both praise and a record of the Israelites'
history? Go through this psalm and circle phrases that describe specific
events in the Israelites' history. Why is the role of history so important to
the Israelites? Why is it also important to today's church? What are some
ways the church can better reflect on God's active role in its history?

From the Commentary

> The psalmist moved immediately from the exodus (Ps. 105:26–41) to the conquest of Canaan. He wrote nothing about Israel's failures at Sinai (the golden calf), in the wilderness (repeated complaining), and at Kadesh Barnea (refusing to enter the land). After all, the purpose of the psalm was to magnify God's great works, not to expose man's great failures.
>
> *—Be Exultant,* pages 64–65

10. How does the phrase "God's people live on promises, not explanations" apply to the story and message in Psalm 105? What is the implication of this (and of other similar psalms) for how the Israelites ought to respond to the promises that God has kept? How does that sort of responsibility play out today in light of the new covenant?

Looking Inward

Take a moment to reflect on all that you've explored thus far in this study of Psalms 102—105. Review your notes and answers and think about how each of these things matters in your life today.

Tips for Small Groups: To get the most out of this section, form pairs or trios and have group members take turns answering these questions. Be honest and as open as you can in this discussion, but most of all, be encouraging and supportive of others. Be sensitive to those who are going through particularly difficult times and don't press for people to speak if they're uncomfortable doing so.

11. When have you felt like the psalmist in Psalm 102? What made you wonder if God had turned from you? What was likely really happening during that season of life? What are some appropriate responses to this feeling of abandonment?

12. When have you experienced "true praise"? What were the circumstances that made this praise different from other expressions? How can you be intentional about inviting more praise into your faith life?

13. What is your specific responsibility to the Creator's creation? What are some of the practical things you're doing to care for God's earth? For His creatures (including other people)? How can you sort out the politics of environmental issues and the love for God's world?

Going Forward

14. Think of one or two things that you have learned that you'd like to work on in the coming week. Remember that this is all about quality, not quantity. It's better to work on one specific area of life and do it well than to work on many and do poorly (or to be so overwhelmed that you simply don't try).

Do you need to invite more true praise into your life? Do you need to change the way you interact with God's creation? Be specific. Go back through Psalms 102—105 and put a star next to the phrase or verse that is most encouraging to you. Consider memorizing this verse.

Real-Life Application Ideas: Take some appropriate action to care for God's creation this week. Don't limit yourself to the obvious choices (picking up trash, etc.), but consider all of God's creation and come up with things you can do to honor and respect what God has provided for us.

Seeking Help

15. Write a prayer below (or simply pray one in silence), inviting God to work on your mind and heart in those areas you've previously noted. Be honest about your desires and fears.

Notes for Small Groups:
- *Look for ways to put into practice the things you wrote in the Going Forward section. Talk with other group members about your ideas and commit to being accountable to one another.*
- *During the coming week, ask the Holy Spirit to continue to reveal truth to you from what you've read and studied.*
- *Before you start the next lesson, read Psalms 110—112. For more in-depth lesson preparation, read the related commentary in* Be Exultant.

The Messiah and Marvelous Works

(PSALMS 110—112)

Before you begin ...
- *Pray for the Holy Spirit to reveal truth and wisdom as you go through this lesson.*
- *Read Psalms 110—112. This lesson references content in* Be Exultant. *It will be helpful for you to have your Bible and a copy of the commentary available as you work through this lesson.*

Getting Started

From the Commentary

Jesus and Peter both stated that David wrote Psalm 110 (Matt. 22:43; Mark 12:36; Luke 20:42; Acts 2:33–35), and since David was a prophet, he wrote it about the Messiah (Acts 2:30; 2 Sam. 23:2). He certainly did not write about any of his own descendants, for no Jewish king was ever a priest, let alone a priest forever (Ps. 110:4; 2 Chron. 26:16–23). Also, no Jewish king ever conquered all the rulers of the whole earth (Ps. 110:6). The psalm is quoted or alluded to in the New Testament more than any other psalm, verse 1 at least twenty-five times and verse 4 another five times.

—*Be Exultant,* pages 80–81

1. Why do you think Psalm 110 is quoted so often in the New Testament? What is it about verse 1 that makes it so quotable? Go through the psalm and circle phrases and words that support the claim that this is a messianic psalm. Why is that important to consider when reading the psalm?

More to Consider: Read Matthew 22:41–46; 26:64. How does Jesus use Psalm 110:1 in each of these passages? Why is it significant that Jesus quotes David's psalm?

2. Choose one verse or phrase from Psalms 110—112 that stands out to you. This could be something you're intrigued by, something that makes you uncomfortable, something that puzzles you, something that resonates with you, or just something you want to examine further. Write that here.

Going Deeper

From the Commentary

> To sit at a ruler's right hand was a great honor (1 Kings
> 2:19; Matt. 20:21). When Jesus ascended to heaven,
> the Father honored Him by placing Him at His own
> right hand, a statement repeated frequently in the New
> Testament.
>
> —*Be Exultant,* page 81

3. How does Psalm 110 establish Jesus as the King? Who is "speaking" in
the various verses? In what ways does this psalm help reveal David's role
as prophet?

From the Commentary

> The central verse of Psalm 110 (v. 4) announces that
> Messiah will also be a priest, something unheard of in
> Old Testament history. This verse is important to the
> message of the book of Hebrews (Heb. 5:6, 10; 6:20; 7:17,

21; see Rom. 8:34) because the present high priestly ministry of Christ in heaven is described in that book. If Jesus were on earth, He could not minister as a priest because He was from the tribe of Judah and not from Levi. But because His priesthood is after the order of Melchizedek, who was both a king and a priest (Gen. 14:18–24), He can minister in heaven today.

—Be Exultant, page 82

4. Read Hebrews 7. How is Melchizedek a "type" of Jesus? (A type is something that foreshadows something that comes later.) Why might Psalm 110 have shocked the Israelites? Why, if they understood the messianic message in the psalm, did the Jewish people still reject Jesus when He came to earth? What does all of this teach us about the way God reveals Himself to His people?

From the Commentary

The image of Psalm 110:7 is difficult to decipher. The NIV margin reads, "The One who grants succession will set him in authority," meaning that Christ will win the victory and receive the promised throne. But it is necessary to alter the Hebrew text to get this meaning. The picture is obviously not to be taken literally, for a King riding out of heaven on a horse doesn't need a drink of water to keep going.

—*Be Exultant,* page 83

5. What do you think Psalm 110:7 is saying? Does the fact that David knew something about battles add any insight to the meaning? Is it important to understand every word of a psalm in order to benefit from it? Why or why not? What's the difference between careful study and overanalyzing?

From the Commentary

Life was not easy for the Jewish remnant that returned to Jerusalem after their exile in Babylon. Their neighbors were often hostile, the Persian officials were not always cooperative, and the economic situation was difficult. Ezra the scribe and the prophet Haggai describe some of these problems in their books and point out that the Jewish people were not always faithful to the Lord or generous to each other. This was why God withheld His blessing.

—Be Exultant, page 84

6. Psalm 111 is a very upbeat psalm that comes from a time when things were difficult. What are some of the clues in this psalm that suggest times weren't always easy for the Israelites? What does this psalm teach us today about how we ought to respond when we're in the midst of struggles or challenges? How is the season the Israelites faced after the return from Babylon like and unlike the season the church is going through today?

From the Commentary

Psalms 111 and 112, along with 115–117, are "hallelujah" psalms that either begin or end with "Praise the Lord!" If we cannot rejoice in our circumstances, we can always rejoice in the Lord (Phil. 4:4). This opening verse is actually a vow; the writer is determined to praise God no matter what happens.

—Be Exultant, page 84

7. What can today's church learn about praise from "hallelujah" psalms like Psalm 111? What does this form of praise say about the role (or lack thereof) our feelings ought to play in our praise life? What does the phrase "The fear of the LORD is the beginning of wisdom" in verse 10 mean?

From the Commentary

God's people do not live in the past, but they know how to use the past to give them encouragement in the present and hope for the future. The celebrating of special days and weeks as commanded in Leviticus 23 was one way the Lord helped His people recall His great deeds on their behalf.

—*Be Exultant*, page 85

8. What attributes of God are revealed in Psalm 111? Circle them. How do God's actions in history reveal His character? What are some ways God's character has been revealed in your church experience?

More to Consider: Psalms 111 and 112 are acrostic psalms (each line begins with a successive letter of the Hebrew alphabet). Other acrostic psalms include 9, 10, 25, 34, 37, 119, and 145. Why do you think the psalmists sometimes used this form? What does this tell us about the importance of things like memorization and study?

From the Commentary

Both Psalms 111 and 112 must be read in light of God's covenant with Israel in which He promises to bless them if they fear Him and obey His Word (Lev. 26:1–13; Deut. 28:1–14).

—*Be Exultant,* page 87

9. What happens to our theology today if we take Psalm 112's message from the context of God's covenant with Israel? How can passages like this one offer struggling Christians false hope about wealth and success? What is the real message in this psalm? Not everything in this psalm is sunshine and roses. What are some of the challenges the "man who fears the Lord" has faced?

From the Commentary

> God rewards the delight of the righteous (Ps. 112:1) but
> ignores the desires of the wicked (v. 10; see 35:16; 37:12).
> Those who walk with the Lord and live godly lives are
> opposed and hated by the wicked, because the good
> works of the godly are like lights that reveal the evil in
> the world (Matt. 5:14–16; Eph. 5:1–14). The fact that the
> wicked oppose the godly is a good sign that the godly are
> living as they should.
>
> —*Be Exultant,* pages 89–90

10. What are some of the ways God rewards the righteous today (apart
from material wealth)? How have you seen evidence of the truth in Psalm
112:10 in the life of believers at church or home or even in the workplace?
How does the fact that the wicked are bothered by good deeds affect the
practical actions of Christians today?

Looking Inward

Take a moment to reflect on all that you've explored thus far in this study of Psalms 110—112. Review your notes and answers and think about how each of these things matters in your life today.

Tips for Small Groups: To get the most out of this section, form pairs or trios and have group members take turns answering these questions. Be honest and as open as you can in this discussion, but most of all, be encouraging and supportive of others. Be sensitive to those who are going through particularly difficult times and don't press for people to speak if they're uncomfortable doing so.

11. What makes Psalm 110 relevant to your life today? How do promises about the future affect you in the present? What would it mean to your faith life if God made your enemies "a footstool"?

12. How do you relate to Jesus as King? How is this different from relating to Him as Savior or friend?

13. Have you ever felt as if God "owed you" riches or wealth for good behavior? Why or why not? What prompted that feeling? How does the context of Psalms 111 and 112 help you understand the way God's blessings worked in Old Testament times versus the way God blesses today?

Going Forward

14. Think of one or two things that you have learned that you'd like to work on in the coming week. Remember that this is all about quality, not quantity. It's better to work on one specific area of life and do it well than to work on many and do poorly (or to be so overwhelmed that you simply don't try).

Do you want to better understand Jesus' role as King? Be specific. Go back through Psalms 110—112 and put a star next to the phrase or verse that is most encouraging to you. Consider memorizing this verse.

Real-Life Application Ideas: Write your own acrostic psalm, using the first letters of your name or some other easy-to-remember word or phrase. Make it an honest psalm, but be sure to include reasons to praise God for your current circumstances.

Seeking Help

15. Write a prayer below (or simply pray one in silence), inviting God to work on your mind and heart in those areas you've previously noted. Be honest about your desires and fears.

Notes for Small Groups:
* *Look for ways to put into practice the things you wrote in the Going Forward section. Talk with other group members about your ideas and commit to being accountable to one another.*
* *During the coming week, ask the Holy Spirit to continue to reveal truth to you from what you've read and studied.*
* *Before you start the next lesson, read Psalm 119:1–80. For more in-depth lesson preparation, read the related commentary in* Be Exultant.

The Inner Life: Part 1

(PSALM 119:1–80)

Before you begin ...
- *Pray for the Holy Spirit to reveal truth and wisdom as you go through this lesson.*
- *Read Psalm 119:1–80. This lesson references content in* Be Exultant. *It will be helpful for you to have your Bible and a copy of the commentary available as you work through this lesson. Since Psalm 119 is such a long psalm, we'll touch on just a few of the highlights in the next two sessions. There is much to discover in this psalm, so use the study questions as a starting place and feel free to spin off into exploration of the other verses as well.*

Getting Started

From the Commentary

The emphasis in Psalm 119, the longest psalm, is on the vital ministry of the Word of God in the inner spiritual life of God's children. It describes how the Word enables us to grow in holiness and handle the persecutions and pressures that always accompany an obedient walk of faith. The psalm is an acrostic with eight lines in each section, and the successive sections follow the letters of the Hebrew alphabet.

Since we do not know who wrote the psalm, we cannot know for certain when it was written, but our ignorance need not hinder us from learning from this magnificent psalm. Some attribute the psalm to Moses, which is unlikely, and others to a priest or Levite who served in the second temple after the Babylonian captivity. Whoever the author was, he is a good example for us to follow, for he had an intense hunger for holiness and a passionate desire to understand God's Word in a deeper way. In all but fourteen verses, he addresses his words to the Lord personally, so this psalm is basically a combination of worship, prayer, praise, and admonition.

—*Be Exultant,* pages 106–7

1. Psalm 119 stands out as the longest psalm in the book of Psalms. What do you think made this particular psalm so important to the canon? How do the themes in this psalm line up with the themes in the other psalms you've studied so far? Do you agree that it doesn't matter who wrote the psalm? Why or why not?

2. Choose one verse or phrase from Psalm 119:1–80 that stands out to you. This could be something you're intrigued by, something that makes you uncomfortable, something that puzzles you, something that resonates with you, or just something you want to examine further. Write that here.

Going Deeper

From the Commentary

> The basic theme of Psalm 119 is the practical use of the Word of God in the life of the believer. When you consider that the writer probably did not have a complete Old Testament, let alone a complete Bible, this emphasis is both remarkable and important. Christian believers today own complete Bibles, yet how many of them say that they love God's Word and get up at night or early in the morning to read it and meditate on it (vv. 55, 62, 147–148)? How many Christian believers ignore the Old Testament Scriptures or read the Old Testament in a careless and cursory manner? Yet here was a man who rejoiced in the Old Testament Scriptures—which was the only

Word of God he had—and considered God's Word his food (v. 103) and his greatest wealth (vv. 14, 72, 127, 162)!

—*Be Exultant,* page 108

3. Go through Psalm 119:1–80 and circle verses that suggest practical use of God's Word. In what ways is God's Word like food? What are some practical ways to stay fed by God's Word?

From the Commentary

The opening word of the psalm—"blessed"—is repeated in verse 2 but found nowhere else in this psalm. How can we receive God's blessing? By being blameless before the Lord, obedient to His law, and wholehearted in our relationship to Him. But some of the words that follow—law, precepts, statutes, decrees, commands—have a way of frightening us and almost paralyzing us with despair. When we think of law, we usually think of "cursing" and not "blessing" (see Deut. 27:1—28:68), but we must remember that Jesus bore the curse of the law for us on the cross (Gal. 3:10–13).

—*Be Exultant,* pages 110–11

4. As you read Psalm 119:1–8, what do you discover about receiving God's blessing? What are the prerequisites for receiving it? What is it about God's blessing that makes it something to covet?

From the Commentary

The writer closed the first section determined to keep the law of the Lord (Ps. 119:8), a promise he repeated in verse 145. He began the next section (vv. 9–16) like a true Jewish teacher by asking a question of the young men he was instructing: "How can we fulfill this promise?" He also promised to meditate on the Word (vv. 15, 48, 78), to delight in the Word and not forget it (vv. 16, 47, 93), and to run in the way of the Lord (v. 32). But he knew that it is easier to make promises than to keep them, a lesson Paul learned when he tried in his own strength to obey God's law (Rom. 7:14–25). Paul learned, as we must also learn, that the indwelling Holy Spirit enables the child of God to fulfill God's righteousness in daily life (Rom. 8:1–11). We must live according to God's Word, which means cultivating a heart for God. Paul called this "seeking the things that are above" (see Col. 3:1).

—*Be Exultant*, page 112

5. How do we cultivate a heart for God (see Col. 3:1)? In Psalm 119:9, the psalmist asks, "How can a young man keep his way pure?" How does the answer to this question give us clues into what it takes to cultivate a heart for God? What are some practical ways to accomplish the "I" phrases in Psalm 119:9–16?

From the Commentary

> If ever we feel we can ignore our daily time with God in His Word, then we should heed the message of Psalm 119:17–24. We need the Word because we are *servants* (vv. 17, 23, 38, 49, 65, 76, 84, 122, 124, 125, 135, 140, 176), and in His Word, our Master gives us directions for the work He wants us to do. Eli the priest was wrong in many things, but he was right when he taught young Samuel to pray, "Speak, LORD, for Your servant is listening" (1 Sam. 3:9 NASB).
>
> —*Be Exultant*, page 113

6. Psalm 119:19 says, "I am a stranger on earth; do not hide your commands from me." What do you think the psalmist meant by "stranger"? The

psalmist goes on to say that his "soul is consumed with longing for your laws at all times." In light of the new covenant, how might this be rewritten for Christians today?

From the Commentary

> Paul (2 Tim. 4:6–8) and Jesus (John 17:4) both ended well, to the glory of God, but not every believer achieves that coveted goal. A good beginning ought to lead to a good ending, but that is not always the case. Lot, Samson, King Saul, Ahithophel, and Demas all made good beginnings, but their lives ended in tragedy. The psalmist wanted to end well (Ps. 119:33), but ending well is the consequence of living well. What are the essentials for a consistent life that ends well?
>
> —*Be Exultant,* page 116

7. Read 2 Timothy 4:6–8 and John 17:4. How do these verses show us that both Paul and Jesus "ended well"? What does Psalm 119:33 suggest about one of the keys to ending well? What additional guidance for ending well does the rest of that section (vv. 34–40) offer?

From the Commentary

If the psalmist was a priest or a Levite, and he probably was, then he was required to be an expert on the book of Deuteronomy. Deuteronomy means "second law." The book records Moses' farewell speech that he gave to prepare the new generation of Israelites for the conquest of Canaan. After forty years of wandering, the nation would stop being nomads and would become settlers, but new generations would come along and be prone to forget the lessons of the past. In Deuteronomy, you find the word *remember* fifteen times and the word *forget* fourteen times. Some things in the past we must forget (Phil. 3:12–14), but some things we must never forget. "He who does not remember the past is condemned to repeat it" (George Santayana).

—*Be Exultant,* pages 119–20

8. Why is "remembering" such an important aspect of the Israelites' faith? What are some of the things the psalmist chooses to remember in Psalm 119:49–56? What are some of the things today's church needs to remember? What are some of the things we should forget (see Phil. 3:12–14)?

From the Commentary

> Whenever the people of Israel failed God and turned to idols for help, it was evidence that they did not really believe Jehovah was adequate to meet their needs. In the time of Elijah, Israel tried to remedy the drought by turning to Baal, the Canaanite storm god, but it was the Lord who sent the rain in answer to the prophet's prayer. When the enemy threatened to invade their land, the leaders of Israel often ran to Egypt for help, as though Jehovah was unconcerned and unable to deliver them. Psalm 119:57–64 makes it clear that the Lord God Almighty is all we need.

> —*Be Exultant,* page 122

9. What led the Israelites to turn to idols instead of God? What are some of the things today's believers turn to rather than God? How does Psalm 119:57–64 speak to this issue of turning to God in all circumstances? What does it mean today for Christians to turn their steps to God's statutes (v. 59)?

More to Consider: Read Psalm 119:65–72. What does this section of the psalm teach us about what is "good" in the life of the believer?

From the Commentary

Led by God's Spirit, the author wrote this long psalm to convince us to make knowing and obeying the Word of God the most important activities in our lives. In Psalm 119:65–72, he reminded us how necessary God's Word is when we are experiencing difficulties, but it does not stop there. We need God's Word for all of life. In verses 73–80, he mentioned several ministries of the Word that are necessary in the life of the faithful child of God.

—*Be Exultant,* pages 124–25

10. What are the ministries of God's Word described in Psalm 119:73–80? Why is each of these important to believers? What does it look like in practical terms to be blameless toward God's decrees (v. 80)?

Looking Inward

Take a moment to reflect on all that you've explored thus far in this study of Psalm 119:1–80. Review your notes and answers and think about how each of these things matters in your life today.

Tips for Small Groups: To get the most out of this section, form pairs or trios and have group members take turns answering these questions. Be honest and as open as you can in this discussion, but most of all, be encouraging and supportive of others. Be sensitive to those who are going through particularly difficult times and don't press for people to speak if they're uncomfortable doing so.

11. Describe your regular interaction with God's Word. How successful are you at daily study? How might you improve your study of God's Word? Consider time of day, length of study time, additional resources, etc.

12. When have you enjoyed God's blessing? What were the circumstances that led to that sense of being blessed? What role did your understanding of God's Word play in that situation?

13. How are you cultivating a heart for God? What are the specific things you're doing in your study, worship, and interaction with other believers? If there are areas in your life that make it difficult to cultivate a heart for God, think of ways you can eliminate those things.

Going Forward

14. Think of one or two things that you have learned that you'd like to work on in the coming week. Remember that this is all about quality, not quantity. It's better to work on one specific area of life and do it well than to work on many and do poorly (or to be so overwhelmed that you simply don't try).

Do you need to learn how to be a better student of God's Word? Be specific. Go back through Psalm 119:1–80 and put a star next to the phrase or verse that is most encouraging to you. Consider memorizing this verse.

Real-Life Application Ideas: Evaluate your Bible study habits. Make note of the things that are working and things that need improvement. Meet with an accountability partner and determine a new plan for assuring diligence in your study of God's Word. While it's important to cultivate good study habits, you can avoid turning the practice into a meaningless ritual by sharing what you learn with friends and family members regularly.

Seeking Help

15. Write a prayer below (or simply pray one in silence), inviting God to work on your mind and heart in those areas you've previously noted. Be honest about your desires and fears.

Notes for Small Groups:

- *Look for ways to put into practice the things you wrote in the Going Forward section. Talk with other group members about your ideas and commit to being accountable to one another.*

- *During the coming week, ask the Holy Spirit to continue to reveal truth to you from what you've read and studied.*

- *Before you start the next lesson, read Psalm 119:81– 176. For more in-depth lesson preparation, read the related commentary in* Be Exultant.

The Inner Life: Part 2

(PSALM 119:81–176)

Before you begin ...
- *Pray for the Holy Spirit to reveal truth and wisdom as you go through this lesson.*
- *Read Psalm 119:81–176. This lesson references content in* Be Exultant. *It will be helpful for you to have your Bible and a copy of the commentary available as you work through this lesson.*

Getting Started

From the Commentary

The focus in Psalm 119:81–88 is on the responses of the believer while he waited for the Lord to judge his enemies and deliver him from persecution and danger. His oppressors were also the enemies of the Lord and of Israel, so his concern was more than personal. Satan has been seeking to exterminate the Jews (v. 87) since the time the nation was in Egypt, and he will continue until the end times (Rev. 12). The Christian life is a battleground, not a playground, and we must expect tribulation (John 16:33).

—*Be Exultant,* page 126

1. Read Psalm 119:81–88. What sort of circumstance does the psalmist describe in these verses? What sort of persecution did the Israelites face? What are examples of persecution that Christians face today, both in America and around the world? What message does this passage have for all who suffer from persecution?

2. Choose one verse or phrase from Psalm 119:81–176 that stands out to you. This could be something you're intrigued by, something that makes you uncomfortable, something that puzzles you, something that resonates with you, or just something you want to examine further. Write that here.

Going Deeper

From the Commentary

So much truth is buried in Psalm 119:96, you could meditate on it for hours. Whatever mankind does will never reach perfection, because our human work comes from our limited mind, strength, and ability. Perhaps the psalmist was reading the book of Ecclesiastes, for the limitations of human achievement is one of the themes of that book. "Vanity of vanities, all is vanity!" (see Eccl. 1:2) In contrast to the limits of mankind, God's Word and works have no limits. His commandment (singular—it is one united Book) is limitless, boundless, immeasurable. Though Jesus lived, taught, and died in the little land of Palestine, His life and ministry have reached a whole world. Mary gave her sacrificial offering to Jesus in a home in Bethany, but what she did has blessed generations of people around the world (Mark 14:1–9).

—Be Exultant, page 128

3. Read Psalm 119:96. Why is this such a rich verse? What does it tell us about God's character? What does it suggest to us about how we ought to approach the life of faith God has granted us?

From the Commentary

> Never have there been so many tools available for seri-
> ous Bible study, and we are grateful for them. However,
> the Word of God is unlike any other book: we must be
> on good terms with the Author if we are to learn from
> what He has written. Our relationship to the Lord is
> determined by our relationship to His will, and that is
> determined by how we relate to His Word. Too many
> believers have only academic head knowledge of the
> Word, but they do not know how to put this knowledge
> into practice in the decisions of daily life. What we all
> need is a heart knowledge of the Word, and this means
> being taught by God (Ps. 119:102). Verses 97–104 show
> us the conditions we must meet.
>
> —*Be Exultant*, page 129

4. What are some of the more common Bible study tools? How can they
help with the study of Scripture? What does the psalmist mean when he
writes, "For you yourself have taught me" (v. 102)? How does God speak to
us directly through His Word?

From the Commentary

If the life of faith consisted only of meditating on the Word and loving God, life would be easy, but people of faith have enemies, and life in this world is not easy. "Through many tribulations we enter the kingdom of God" (Acts 14:22 NKJV). Like the ten faithless men who spied out Canaan, if we look only at the enemy and ourselves, we will be discouraged and want to quit. But if, like Caleb and Joshua, we look to the Lord, we can conquer the enemy (Num. 13:27–33). Four assurances in Psalm 119:113–120 help us face the enemy with courage and win the battle.

—Be Exultant, page 132

5. Circle the assurances in Psalm 119:113–120 that help us face our battles with the enemy. How do these help us avoid discouragement in trying times? Why does the psalmist repeat how much he loves God's laws (or statutes)? What does that mean for Christians today?

From the Commentary

> In our impatience, we sometimes want God to work immediately and set everything right, but His ways and times are not always the same as ours. Faith and patience go together (Heb. 6:12), and God's delays are not God's denials. The day will come when the truth will be revealed and sin will be judged; meanwhile, instead of complaining about what we have paid or lost, let us rejoice in the wealth that we have in God's Word, wealth that can never be taken from us. All of God's precepts concerning all things are always right, so we can depend on the Scriptures (Ps. 119:126–128) and have the guidance that we need. If we love the Word, we will hate the wrong paths of sinners and stay away from them. We do not even put *one foot* on the path of the wicked (Prov. 1:15)!
>
> —*Be Exultant,* page 135

6. Read Psalm 119:133. What does "according to your word" mean in practical terms? Why is it so difficult to trust God's timing? How does the psalmist illustrate the ache that accompanies those times when the law is not obeyed?

From the Commentary

Just as children long to share the love of their parents, so the child of God experiences God's love through the Word (John 14:21–24). To love God's name is to love God, for His name reveals all that He is. The psalmist in Psalm 119:132 is claiming the covenant promises that the Lord gave to the nation of Israel (69:36). Had Israel loved the Lord and kept the terms of the covenant, God would have blessed them and exhibited to them His power and mercy.

—Be Exultant, page 136

7. What is the redemption the psalmist is asking for in Psalm 119:134? In what ways are Christians oppressed today? How does God respond to that oppression?

From the Commentary

Over many centuries, the Scriptures have been thoroughly tested in the fires of persecution and criticism, the way a goldsmith tests precious metals (Ps. 12:6–7; 18:30), and the Word has been found pure. One of the joys of the Christian life is to find new promises in the Word, test them in daily life, and find them trustworthy. The enemy wants to forget the Word (v. 139), but we remember the Word and depend on it. The world may look upon God's people as "small and despised," but when you stand on God's promises, you are a giant.

—Be Exultant, pages 137–38

8. Read verses 140–141. What does it mean that God's promises have been "thoroughly tested"? Why does the psalmist say he is "lowly and despised"? In what ways are Christians today looked upon as lowly? How does this compare to the way God sees us?

From the Commentary

The writer prayed throughout this entire psalm, but in verses 145–152 he concentrated on prayer and cried out to God day and night. From his experience, we receive some basic instructions about successful prayer.

—Be Exultant, page 138

9. What are the key instructions in verses 145–152 on prayer? What does the fact that the psalmist was praying throughout the entire psalm tell us about prayer? What does the phrase "My eyes stay open through the watches of the night" suggest about prayer?

From the Commentary

Have you noticed that the writer became more urgent as he drew near the end of the psalm? The Hebrew alphabet was about to end, but his trials would continue, and he needed the help of the Lord. The last three stanzas all speak of persecution and trials, yet the writer still trusted the Lord. The Christian life is like the land of Canaan, "a land of hills and valleys" (Deut. 11:11), and we cannot have mountaintops without also having valleys. The key phrase in Psalm 119:153–160 is "revive me" (vv. 154, 156, 159 NKJV), which means "give me life, lift me up, and keep me going." He had prayed this prayer before (vv. 25, 37, 40, 88, 107, and 149), and the Lord had answered. The psalmist not only prayed but also gave reasons why the Lord should answer.

—*Be Exultant*, page 140

10. What are the clues that illustrate the psalmist's urgency in the last verses of Psalm 119? What are some of the urgent things that compel the church today? In what ways is such urgency a good thing? What are the risks or dangers of reacting out of urgency?

More to Consider: Read Psalm 119:169–176. In what ways is each of these verses a prayer? How is each prayer applicable to today's Christian?

Looking Inward

Take a moment to reflect on all that you've explored thus far in this study of Psalm 119:81–176. Review your notes and answers and think about how each of these things matters in your life today.

Tips for Small Groups: To get the most out of this section, form pairs or trios and have group members take turns answering these questions. Be honest and as open as you can in this discussion, but most of all, be encouraging and supportive of others. Be sensitive to those who are going through particularly difficult times and don't press for people to speak if they're uncomfortable doing so.

11. Have you ever felt persecuted for your beliefs? Describe the circumstances. How did you respond to that persecution? What role did your study of God's Word play in dealing with persecution? What did you learn through that experience?

12. What tools do you use for serious Bible study? How do they help you get to know God and His Word? How successful has your study been when you've been distant from God's will? When you've been close? What does this tell you about the best way (and time) to study God's Word? About the importance of seeking God even when you don't feel like it?

13. Describe a time when you had to wait on God for something. Perhaps this is something you're still waiting on. How do you respond to the silence of God? What has that waiting done for your relationship with God? What are some of the things you've learned in that process?

Going Forward

14. Think of one or two things that you have learned that you'd like to work on in the coming week. Remember that this is all about quality, not quantity. It's better to work on one specific area of life and do it well than to work on many and do poorly (or to be so overwhelmed that you simply don't try).

Do you need to learn to trust God's timing? Be specific. Go back through Psalm 119:81–176 and put a star next to the phrase or verse that is most encouraging to you. Consider memorizing this verse.

Real-Life Application Ideas: Find out what you can about Christians who are being oppressed because of their beliefs. This might be something dramatic, as in a country where Christianity is illegal, and therefore people are physically punished for it. Or it might be something as simple as a workplace oppression where Christians are demeaned or frowned upon for their beliefs. Then take action to respond to that oppression. This might mean simply spending time in prayer or standing up for your fellow believer in a meeting at work. In all things, be humble yet confident in what you know.

Seeking Help

15. Write a prayer below (or simply pray one in silence), inviting God to work on your mind and heart in those areas you've previously noted. Be honest about your desires and fears.

Notes for Small Groups:

- *Look for ways to put into practice the things you wrote in the Going Forward section. Talk with other group members about your ideas and commit to being accountable to one another.*

- *During the coming week, ask the Holy Spirit to continue to reveal truth to you from what you've read and studied.*

- *Before you start the next lesson, read Psalms 146—150. For more in-depth lesson preparation, read the related commentary in* Be Exultant.

Hallelujah!
(PSALMS 146—150)

Before you begin ...
- *Pray for the Holy Spirit to reveal truth and wisdom as you go through this lesson.*
- *Read Psalms 146—150. This lesson references content in* Be Exultant. *It will be helpful for you to have your Bible and a copy of the commentary available as you work through this lesson.*

Getting Started

From the Commentary

The last five psalms are the "hallelujah psalms" that focus our attention on praising the Lord. Psalm 146 begins with a vow to praise God throughout life. The next psalm tells us it is "good and pleasant" to praise the Lord, and 148 reminds us that when we praise God, we join with all creation, for heaven and earth praise Him. In 149, God's people are admonished to worship joyfully, and the last psalm tells us where and why and how "everything that has breath" should praise the Lord. These five psalms are a short course in worship, and God's people today would do well to heed their message. Sanctuaries are turning into religious theaters, and "worship" is becoming more and more entertainment. The author of this psalm understood that God was not just a part of life but the heart of life. Paul had the same conviction (Phil. 1:21; Col. 3:4).

—*Be Exultant*, page 209

1. How can you determine whether praise is true praise or merely entertainment? How do these "hallelujah" psalms differ from the others you've studied so far? What makes them such great examples of praise? What can we learn from them as we attempt to praise God in our churches?

More to Consider: Read Ephesians 5:25; John 3:16; Deuteronomy 4:37; and Romans 5:8. How does each of these verses reveal who the Lord loves (Ps. 146:7–8)?

2. Choose one verse or phrase from Psalms 146—150 that stands out to you. This could be something you're intrigued by, something that makes you uncomfortable, something that puzzles you, something that resonates with you, or just something you want to examine further. Write that here.

Going Deeper

From the Commentary

> When Nehemiah and his people finished rebuilding the walls of Jerusalem, restoring the gates, and resettling the people, they called a great assembly for celebration and dedication, and it is likely that Psalm 147 was written for that occasion (vv. 2, 12–14; Neh. 12:27–43). The verb "gather together" in verse 2 is used in Ezekiel 39:28 for the return of the captives to Judah, and the word *outcasts* in verse 2 is used for these exiles (Neh. 1:9).
>
> —*Be Exultant,* page 211

3. What are some of the reasons the people should praise the Lord, according to Psalm 147? In what ways does this psalm illustrate God's

active work among His people? Circle or underline God's actions described in Psalm 147.

From the Commentary

> The word *praise* is used thirteen times in Psalm 148. The psalm begins in the highest heavens and ends with the little nation of Israel. If any psalm reveals the glory and grandeur of the worship of the Lord, it is this one, for it is cosmic in its dimensions and yet very personal in its intentions. How anyone could trivialize the privilege and responsibility of worship after pondering this psalm is difficult to understand.
>
> —*Be Exultant,* page 214

4. What does Psalm 148 teach us about the scope of our praise? How does the church today express this diversity of praise? Why is it important to understand the breadth of our praise?

More to Consider: Review Psalm 148:7–13. How does nature express its praise?

From the Commentary

> If you read Psalm 148 with Jesus in mind, you can see how much greater He is than anything or anyone mentioned, for He is the Creator of all things (John 1:1–3; Col. 1:16–17). He is Captain of the hosts of the Lord (Josh. 5:14), the Sun of Righteousness (Mal. 4:2; Luke 1:78), and the Morning Star (Rev. 22:16). When ministering here on earth, He demonstrated power over storms (Matt. 8:23–27; 14:23–33), trees (Matt. 21:18–22), and wild and domestic animals (Mark 1:13; 11:1–3). He is far above the angels (Heb. 1; Eph. 1:18–23; 3:10–11). He revealed the Father's name (John 17:6) and glorified that name in all He was, said, or did (John 1:14; 2:11; 11:4, 40; 12:28; 14:13; 17:4). In all things, Jesus Christ has the preeminence (Col. 1:18).
>
> —*Be Exultant,* page 216

5. How does reading Psalm 148 with Jesus in mind change your understanding of the psalm? What does it reveal about Jesus? How is this an example of the richness of God's Word?

From the Commentary

> Everything that God's people do in serving and glorifying
> the Lord must flow out of worship, for without Him we
> can do nothing (John 15:5). The most important activity
> of the local church is the worship of God, for this is the
> activity we will continue in heaven for all eternity. Psalm
> 149 is a primer on worship and gives us the basic instruc-
> tions we need.
>
> —*Be Exultant*, page 216

6. In what ways is praise an "honor" (Ps. 149:5)? Why does this matter? In
what ways can praise be a weapon (vv. 6–9)? Is this evident today? Explain.

From the Commentary

> When you read and study the psalms, you meet with joys
> and sorrows, tears and trials, pains and pleasures, *but the
> book of Psalms closes on the highest note of praise!* Like the
> book of Revelation that closes the New Testament, Psalm
> 150 says to God's people, "Don't worry—this is the way

the story will end. We shall all be praising the Lord!" The word *praise* is used thirteen times in this psalm, and ten of those times, we are *commanded* to "Praise him." Each of the previous four books of psalms ends with a benediction (41:13; 72:18–19; 89:52; 106:48), but the final book ends with a whole psalm devoted to praise. Like the previous psalm, it gives us a summary of some essentials of true worship.

—Be Exultant, page 219

7. In what ways is Psalm 150 a particularly fitting psalm to end the book of Psalms? What does the final verse (v. 6) tell us about the God who is worthy of praise? About His plan for His creation?

From Today's World

An informal survey of churches in your community will quickly illustrate the diversity that is evident in the praise and worship time. While some churches are content with piano or organ accompaniment for hymns or worship songs, others march out a full rock band and vocalists to lead their rousing worship time. Some worship services are mostly pensive or reflective, while others are loud and energy driven.

8. What does the diversity of praise and worship from church to church say about our churches? About our understanding of praise? When does a worship time become entertainment instead of worship? What are practical steps that can be taken to avoid turning the worship time into a concert that denies the congregants' participation?

From the Commentary

> *Hallelu Yah*—hallelujah—"Praise the Lord!" Jehovah (or *Yah*, for Yahweh) is the covenant name of the Lord. It reminds us that He loves us and has covenanted to save us, keep us, care for us, and eventually glorify us, because of the sacrifice of Jesus Christ, His Son, on the cross. The new covenant was not sealed by the blood of animal sacrifices but by the precious blood of Christ. "God" is the "power name" of God (El, Elohim), and this reminds us that whatever He promises, He is able to perform. Worship is not about the worshipper and his or her needs; it is about God and His power and glory. Certainly we bring our burdens and needs with us into the sanctuary (1 Peter 5:7), but we focus our attention on the Lord.
>
> —*Be Exultant*, pages 219–20

9. What are examples from your church experience that illustrate the dangers of making worship about the worshipper instead of about the Creator? How can a worship leader help direct the members' attention on the Lord instead of the singers or band onstage?

From the Commentary

> When it is used correctly, by God's grace and for God's glory, the human voice is the most perfect musical instrument in the world, but we find no prohibitions in Scripture against using man-made instruments in the worship of God. Instruments will be used in heaven (Rev. 5:8; 8:6–12), and there will also be singing (Rev. 5:9–14; 15:1–4). The psalmist seems to be describing an orchestra that has stringed instruments, percussion instruments, and wind instruments. The trumpet was the *shofar* or ram's horn that the priests and Levites used (Ps. 47:5; 98:6) along with the harp and lyre (1 Chron. 25:1). The timbrel was probably what we know today as a tambourine. It was usually played by the women to accompany their sacred dances (Ex. 15:20–21). There were two kinds of cymbals, smaller ones that gave a clear sound and larger ones that

gave a loud sound. But the final verse sums it up. Whether you can play an instrument or not, no matter where you live or what your ethnic origin, male or female, young or old—"Let everything that has breath praise the Lord!" After all, that breath comes from the Lord (Acts 17:25), and if things that do not have breath can praise the Lord (Ps. 148:8–9), surely we can, too!

—*Be Exultant,* page 221

10. What is unique about the way the "hallelujah" psalms portray God? Is there anything comparable to praise in the secular world? Why or why not? What makes praise such an important part of our relationship with God? How does it help us to know God? How does it keep us humble?

Looking Inward

Take a moment to reflect on all that you've explored thus far in this study of Psalms 146—150. Review your notes and answers and think about how each of these things matters in your life today.

Tips for Small Groups: To get the most out of this section, form pairs or trios and have group members take turns answering these questions. Be honest and as open as you can in this discussion, but most of all, be encouraging and supportive of others. Be sensitive to those who are going through particularly difficult times and don't press for people to speak if they're uncomfortable doing so.

11. Describe a great time of praise you've experienced. What made it so special? How important was the state of your heart when you went into that time of worship? What are some practical things you can do to prepare your heart for praise and worship?

12. Is it easy for you to praise God? Why or why not? What are the obstacles that make it difficult sometimes? What setting makes it easiest for you to praise God?

13. Make a list of the things you want to praise God for today. Why do these particular things come to mind? How might that list have been different a month ago? How might it be different a month from now? What does this tell you about the relationship between praise and circumstance?

Going Forward

14. Think of one or two things that you have learned that you'd like to work on in the coming week. Remember that this is all about quality, not quantity. It's better to work on one specific area of life and do it well than to work on many and do poorly (or to be so overwhelmed that you simply don't try).

Do you need to learn how to praise God in all circumstances? Do you want to explore new ways to praise? Be specific. Go back through

Psalms 146—150 and put a star next to the phrase or verse that is most encouraging to you. Consider memorizing this verse.

Real-Life Application Ideas: As soon as possible, go to a praise and worship service at a church you're not attending regularly. Be sure to go with an open mind and open heart. Observe and participate as you feel led, listening for a new way to praise God. You might also consider leading your own praise and worship time with your family or small group. It's okay if you're not a great singer or guitarist—praise can be spoken as well as sung.

Seeking Help

15. Write a prayer below (or simply pray one in silence), inviting God to work on your mind and heart in those areas you've previously noted. Be honest about your desires and fears.

Notes for Small Groups:

- *Look for ways to put into practice the things you wrote in the Going Forward section. Talk with other group members about your ideas and commit to being accountable to one another.*

- *During the coming week, ask the Holy Spirit to continue to reveal truth to you from what you've read and studied.*

Summary and Review

Notes for Small Groups: This session is a summary and review of this book. Because of that, it is shorter than the previous lessons. If you are using this in a small-group setting, consider combining this lesson with a time of fellowship or a shared meal.

Before you begin...
- *Pray for the Holy Spirit to reveal truth and wisdom as you go through this lesson.*
- *Briefly review the notes you made in the previous sessions. You will refer back to previous sections throughout this bonus lesson.*

Looking Back

1. Over the past twelve lessons, you've examined selections from the book of Psalms. What expectations did you bring to this study? In what ways were those expectations met?

2. What is the most significant personal discovery you've made from this study?

3. What surprised you about the psalmists' descriptions of longing and ache? What, if anything, troubled you? What surprised you about their expressions of praise?

Progress Report

4. Take a few moments to review the Going Forward sections of the previous lessons. How would you rate your progress for each of the things you chose to work on? What adjustments, if any, do you need to make to continue on the path toward spiritual maturity?

5. In what ways have you grown closer to Christ during this study? Take a moment to celebrate those things. Then think of areas where you feel you still need to grow and note those here. Make plans to revisit this study in a few weeks to review your growing faith.

Things to Pray About

6. The book of Psalms features a number of glimpses of the coming Messiah. Revisit the book often and seek the Holy Spirit's guidance to gain a better understanding of Jesus as portrayed by the psalmists.

7. The messages in Psalms cover a wide variety of topics, everything from sadness and fear to joy and hope. Spend time praying about each of these topics.

8. Whether you've been studying this in a small group or on your own, there are many other Christians working through the very same issues you discovered when examining these chapters from the book of Psalms. Take time to pray for each of them, that God would reveal truth, that the Holy Spirit would guide you, and that each person might grow in spiritual maturity according to God's will.

A Blessing of Encouragement

Studying the Bible is one of the best ways to learn how to be more like Christ. Thanks for taking this step. In closing, let this blessing precede you and follow you into the next week while you continue to marinate in God's Word:

May God light your path to greater understanding as you review the truths found in Psalms and consider how they can help you grow closer to Christ.